Seasons of LITERACY

A Monthly Guide to Growing Lifelong Readers and Writers

JOELLEN MCCARTHY & JULIA E. TORRES

Solution Tree | Press

Copyright © 2025 by Solution Tree Press

Materials appearing here are copyrighted. With one exception, all rights are reserved. Readers may reproduce only those pages marked "Reproducible." Otherwise, no part of this book may be reproduced or transmitted in any form or by any means (electronic, photocopying, recording, or otherwise) without prior written permission of the publisher. This book, in whole or in part, may not be included in a large language model, used to train AI, or uploaded into any AI system.

555 North Morton Street
Bloomington, IN 47404
800.733.6786 (toll free) / 812.336.7700
FAX: 812.336.7790
email: info@SolutionTree.com
SolutionTree.com

Visit **go.SolutionTree.com/literacy** to download the free reproducibles in this book.

Printed in the United States of America

LCCN: 2024054161

ISBN: 978-1-962188-33-3

Solution Tree
Jeffrey C. Jones, CEO
Edmund M. Ackerman, President

Solution Tree Press
Publisher: Kendra Slayton
Associate Publisher: Todd Brakke
Acquisitions Director: Hilary Goff
Editorial Director: Laurel Hecker
Art Director: Rian Anderson
Managing Editor: Sarah Ludwig
Copy Chief: Jessi Finn
Production Editor: Gabriella Jones-Monserrate
Copy Editor: Mark Hain
Proofreader: Elijah Oates
Text and Cover Designer: Kelsey Hoover
Content Development Specialist: Amy Rubenstein
Associate Editor: Elijah Oates
Editorial Assistant: Madison Chartier

ACKNOWLEDGMENTS

With gratitude for all of the educators, students, and my own family members for teaching me to make every day count.

Jo Ellen

To my children, both at home and at school. Thank you for being my greatest teachers.

Julia E. Torres

Visit **go.SolutionTree.com/literacy** to download the free reproducibles in this book.

TABLE OF CONTENTS

About the Authors 1
Welcome 5
The Year at a Glance 9

Belonging 11

Important Dates	13
Monthly Planner	14
Inspiration	16
Illumination	16
Investigation	17
Mentor Spotlight: Jacqueline Woodson	17
Weekly Planner	18
August Bookshelves	26
Activities and Instructional Moves	30
End-of-Month Reflection Questions	32

Joy 33

Important Dates	35
Monthly Planner	36
Inspiration	38
Illumination	38
Investigation	39
Mentor Spotlight: Gholdy Muhammad	39
Weekly Planner	40
September Bookshelves	48
Activities and Instructional Moves	52
End-of-Month Reflection Questions	53

v

October

Inquiry 55

Important Dates	57
Monthly Planner	58
Inspiration	60
Illumination	60
Investigation	61
Mentor Spotlight: Melissa Stewart	61
Weekly Planner	62
October Bookshelves	70
Activities and Instructional Moves	74
End-of-Month Reflection Questions	76

November

Justice 77

Important Dates	79
Monthly Planner	80
Inspiration	82
Illumination	83
Investigation	84
Mentor Spotlight: Miranda Paul	85
Weekly Planner	86
November Bookshelves	94
Activities and Instructional Moves	98
End-of-Month Reflection Questions	99

December

Remembrance 101

Important Dates	103
Monthly Planner	104
Inspiration	106
Illumination	106
Investigation	107
Mentor Spotlight: Mihn Lê	107
Weekly Planner	108
December Bookshelves	116
Activities and Instructional Moves	120
End-of-Month Reflection Questions	121

January

Calling 123

Important Dates	125
Monthly Planner	126
Inspiration	128
Illumination	128
Investigation	129
Mentor Spotlight: Joanna Ho	129
Weekly Planner	130
January Bookshelves	138
Activities and Instructional Moves	142
End-of-Month Reflection Questions	143

Liberation 145

Important Dates	147
Monthly Planner	148
Inspiration	150
Illumination	150
Investigation	151
Mentor Spotlight: Felicia Rose Chavez	151
Weekly Planner	152
February Bookshelves	160
Activities and Instructional Moves	164
End-of-Month Reflection Questions	165

Renewal 167

Important Dates	169
Monthly Planner	170
Inspiration	172
Illumination	172
Investigation	173
Mentor Spotlight: Anton Treuer	173
Weekly Planner	174
March Bookshelves	182
Activities and Instructional Moves	186
End-of-Month Reflection Questions	188

Affirmation 189

Important Dates	191
Monthly Planner	192
Inspiration	194
Illumination	194
Investigation	195
Mentor Spotlight: Katie Yamasaki	195
Weekly Planner	196
April Bookshelves	204
Activities and Instructional Moves	208
End-of-Month Reflection Questions	210

Possibility 211

Important Dates	213
Monthly Planner	214
Inspiration	216
Illumination	216
Investigation	217
Mentor Spotlight: Antero Garcia	217
Weekly Planner	218
May Bookshelves	226
Activities and Instructional Moves	230
End-of-Month Reflection Questions	232

June — Play and Rest 233

- Important Dates — 235
- Monthly Planner — 236
- Inspiration — 238
- Illumination — 238
- Investigation — 239
- Mentor Spotlight: Bettina Love — 239
- Weekly Planner — 240
- June Bookshelves — 248
- Activities and Instructional Moves — 252
- End-of-Month Reflection Questions — 254

July — Imagination 255

- Important Dates — 257
- Monthly Planner — 258
- Inspiration — 260
- Illumination — 260
- Investigation — 261
- Mentor Spotlight: Kwame Alexander — 261
- Weekly Planner — 262
- July Bookshelves — 270
- Activities and Instructional Moves — 274
- End-of-Month Reflection Questions — 275

Farewell 277

References and Resources 279

Index 291

ABOUT THE AUTHORS

JoEllen McCarthy is a lifelong learner and educator who started her career in the New York City public schools. She has the privilege of serving students and educators as a visiting teacher, literacy coach, and staff developer. JoEllen is also a National Literacy Advisor for Bookelicious and Book Ambassador with multiple organizations who is recognized for the ways she spreads her enthusiasm for literature, always using inclusive mentor texts and books as co-teachers. Her research and teaching focus on student-centered, responsive pedagogy and practices that recognize students as the most important aspect of the curriculum. She is committed to supporting whole-school communities and works to connect the joy *and* science of reading to all aspects of literacy learning. JoEllen works with the Educator Collaborative, Bookelicious, and various nonprofits. As an advisory board member of the Carol Pufahl Foundation, JoEllen worked to expand literacy and learning opportunities for children, educators, and families in the most underserved communities and schools. Through a collaboration with Dolly Parton's Imagination Library, she has facilitated many family literacy workshops and supported the book gifting program providing a book a month to children from birth to age five. JoEllen continues to make it her aim to get books in the hands of readers of all ages.

As a speaker recognized across North America, JoEllen champions the power of read-alouds and demonstrates the ways we can layer our academic and affective standards for lessons in reading, writing, and life. She explores her vision for this work for teachers, families, and students in her book, *Layers of Learning: Using Read-Alouds to Connect Literacy and Caring Conversations* (2020). JoEllen's work has been featured in publications for the International Literacy Association, National Council of Teachers of English (NCTE), and more.

JoEllen is an expert in children's reading development and rigorous elementary literacy instruction. She is also a founder of the literacy-based EdCamp model nErDcampLI in New York, an annual "unconference" that is a participant-driven learning and networking experience designed for educators and children's literature creators passionate about teaching and learning to promote access and engagement and spread book joy.

JoEllen holds degrees from Loyola University Maryland, New York University, and an administrative degree specializing in staff development from Hofstra University.

Julia E. Torres is a librarian, veteran language arts teacher, and teen programs administrator in Denver, Colorado, recognized across the United States for her work. Julia has been an educator since 2005 and a librarian since 2018. Her focus is on culturally inclusive literacy instruction and incorporating best practices of librarianship within language arts praxis.

Julia specializes in literacy curriculum and instruction for secondary learners and their leaders. She has taught every secondary grade level and was the librarian for five co-located middle and high schools in Denver Public Schools' Far Northeast region. Julia has also taught high school concurrent enrollment courses and served as an adjunct instructor for the Community College of Aurora and Metropolitan State University of Denver. She has national and international experience providing professional development workshops and conference keynotes on the intersections of language arts instruction, culturally responsive librarianship, and more.

Julia is a past president of the Colorado Language Arts Society (a state affiliate of the NCTE). She served as the secondary representative at large for the executive committee of the NCTE from 2018 to 2020. In 2020, Julia was selected to be a Library Journal Mover and Shaker. That same year, she was awarded the title of secondary teacher of the year by the Colorado NCTE affiliate organization. Her coauthored book *Liven Up Your Library: Design Engaging and Inclusive Programs for Teens and Tweens* is just the first of many forthcoming publications for librarians and educators.

Julia holds a master's degree in secondary education curriculum and instruction with a focus on secondary language arts instruction from the University of Phoenix, a master of arts degree in creative writing from Regis University, and a master of library and information science degree from the University of Denver.

To reach out to the authors about all things related to *Seasons of Literacy*, contact LitPlanning365@gmail.com.

To book JoEllen McCarthy or Julia E. Torres for professional development, contact pd@solutiontree.com.

WELCOME

Dear Educators,

Congratulations! You've taken the first step toward what promises to be a year of inspiration and transformation. This planner has been designed first and foremost as a guide to support developing readers and the adults who serve them in every stage of the reading or learning journey. At the time of its creation, we find ourselves at a curious crossroads. We as a global community of educators are seeing unprecedented shifts within our field. These shifts impact us individually and collectively. As two literacy educators who remember what it was like to teach "before" efforts for inclusion became more aware and effective (with over fifty years of collective experience), we wanted to create a resource that is truly for everyone.

Whether you are new to the field of education, helping young people develop a relationship with words in a nontraditional setting, or an experienced educator in search of inspiration and reminders about just why we return to the classroom year after year, think of this planner as the first step on the road to repair that we can travel together. We hope it will be a place you can return to again and again for inspiration, as a record of your personal evolution, and as a reminder about how much this work gives us cause for celebration.

We believe this is the planner you need for daily inspiration and celebration. This engaging, interactive resource will invite new and seasoned educators, as well as all lovers of literacy, to celebrate the process of building a lifelong relationship with words.

This planner is a departure from the plan books of old, in that you will find space to remember all that you love about a life filled with literacy and young people. We have designed the pages of this planner to encourage collaboration and celebration between individuals, young people, and communities who love reading.

In this planner, you will find each month is structured the same way. After the Year at a Glance section, in which you can reimagine your academic year and the personal growth that will happen along the way, each month features the following items and activities.

- **The Important Dates page:** This page provides a list of national holidays and celebrations occurring during the month. We obtained our information for these days from the following sources.
    - The American Legal Association's (n.d.) Diversity Heritage Months calendar
    - The American Library Association's (2007) Library Celebration Days calendar
    - The National Day Calendar (2025)
- **The Monthly Planner pages:** These pages provide you with a glance of the upcoming month. This spread offers space to dream and plan.
- **The Inspiration, Illumination, and Investigation pages:** These pages include actionable invitations for the month based on that month's theme. Each section has its own purpose.
    - **Inspiration:** People do some of their best learning when they are inspired by others. To be inspired, we must explore and be open to encountering ideas that come from lived experiences like our own as well as those that are entirely different. Help young people find inspiration by supporting their experiences and connections with those in their classroom and other communities they call home. This section also introduces you to ideas educators as a whole have adopted and refined over time.
    - **Illumination:** This section will help you develop new insights into students and assist with self-reflective practices. You will find questions that expand on the themes from each month.
    - **Investigation:** This section is a guide to the practices and pedagogies that have been proven to elevate literacy practices, giving you an opportunity to adopt or adapt

from the suggested activities. Investigations include a general overview of how to put monthly themes into practice with your students.

- **The Mentor Spotlight page:** Use the Mentor Spotlight to learn more about the work of celebrated educators and authors and consider perspectives outside of familiar communities and influences. Often, teachers get siloed into learning from the same voices. The Mentor Spotlight introduces new ways of thinking and doing, which can ultimately transform classrooms for the better.

- **The Weekly Planner pages:** Each week in the month has its own double-page spread with ample space to plan your tasks. These pages include weekly inspiring quotes and space to grapple with intriguing ideas from innovators and creators.

- **The Bookshelves pages:** As literacy experts, we lovingly curated our recommendations for cherished titles and educator resources to strengthen, renew, and restore your practice, which you will find on the Bookshelves pages. On the second of these double-page spreads, you'll have a blank "bookshelf" available to record books you used in class or record any recommendations you received from peers.

- **The Activities and Instructional Moves pages:** The Activities and Instructional Moves pages offer ready-to-implement ideas you can use in your classroom setting. These are intended to tie directly to classroom instruction, with the understanding that you have already familiarized yourself with the general overview of the monthly theme.

- **The End-of-Month Reflection Questions page:** At the end of each month, you will encounter a dedicated reflection point with guiding questions to help you draw lessons from the month and plan for the future. Doodle, journal, sketch, or write in the spaces for reflection to have a record of the most pivotal moments in your year.

Educator and author Gloria Anzaldúa once famously stated, "Caminante, no hay puentes, se hace puentes al andar" ("Voyager, there are no bridges, one builds them as one walks;" Moraga & Anzaldúa, 2015, p. 254). And so, we must remember we are building bridges between past and present, forging a future landscape for readers in a time when the right to read in many spaces is not guaranteed. We know that along with celebrating all the riches in stories we love, we must recognize that unprecedented numbers of young people still have to fight for the right to read what, when, and in the forms they choose.

We can work together to create this bold and brave new literacy landscape. Thank you for your heart, for having the courage to show up for young people today and each day, and for choosing this book to guide you along the way. We have heard in our respective careers before, "Always be mentoring someone, and always be vulnerable enough to be mentored." Think of this as a mentor text for your future self and a place to process where you've been, where you are, and where you're headed as you embark on your yearly literary journey. Complete it alone, or in community with your team, class, or family. Plan a month in advance or skip a few days. It's your planner, your path, so do it your way. Are you ready? Good! Let's go.

We are linking arms and walking right beside you. Your first step starts here. Reach out to us at LitPlanning365@gmail.com to stay connected, share your comments, questions and more.

THE YEAR AT A GLANCE

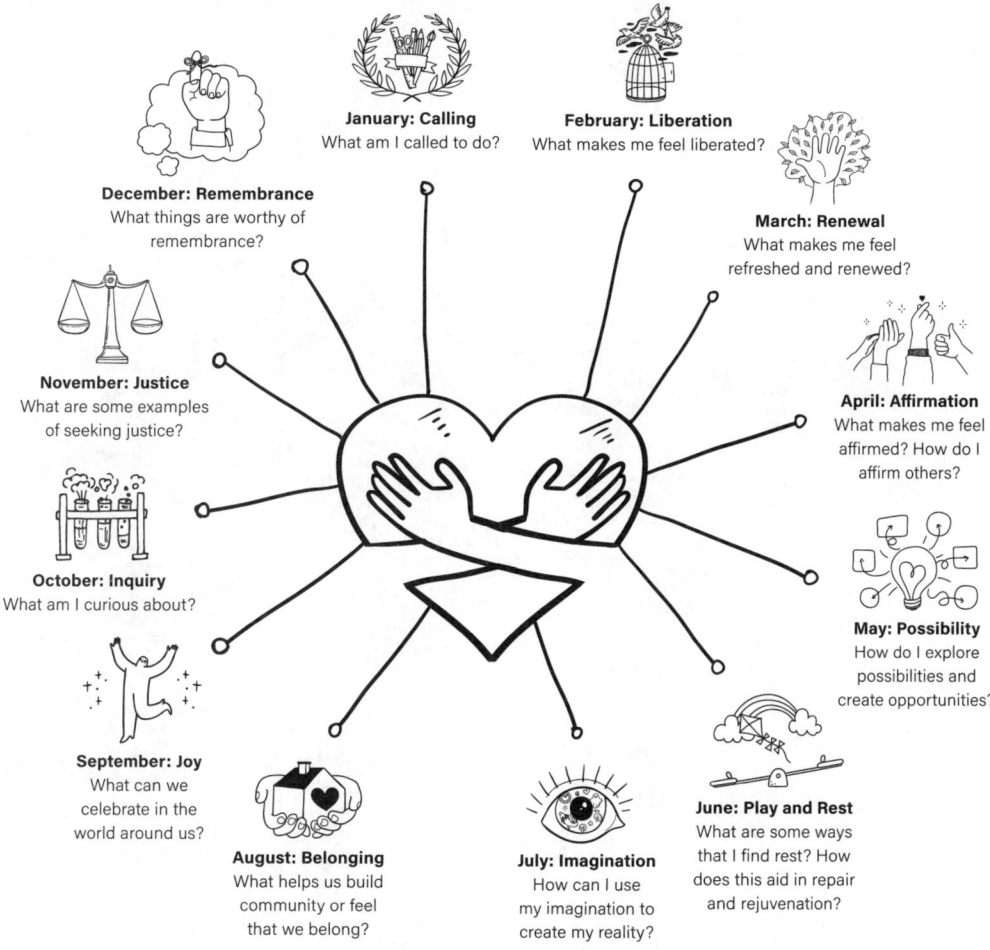

We open this planner with a representation of a full, undated year, beginning in August and ending in July, that you may use during the school year, shown in the image above. Each month carries a specific theme that we relate back to literacy. These monthly themes provide predictable patterns for readers. They also serve as scaffolds for incorporating further learning exploration around connected ideas that support individuals living in and understanding their communities. We also connect the texts we incorporated to the communal experiences we remember having in classrooms, school communities, and society. Ideally, the themes will help readers feel more connected to one another and to the world, as some of the best and most memorable learning is learning done in community.

AUGUST

Belonging

And it's not even strange that it feels the way it's always felt like the place we belong to. Like home.

—Jacqueline Woodson

Don't we all feel the safest, the most confident, and the most able to grow in the places we call home? You may feel a sense of belonging when in a specific place, with a particularly comforting group of people, or while reading a treasured book. This month, we invite you to consider what kinds of spaces make students feel like they belong, and all the good that can come from creating, sustaining, and protecting these spaces.

Belonging is a feeling that can best be described as acceptance in action. We feel belonging in our bodies, hearts, and minds when we are accepted as individuals and know that our contributions and presence are valued. Alternatively, we also know when something indescribably isn't right and we feel we don't belong in a particular group or setting. As educators, one of our most important goals is to create environments and scenarios where all students, regardless of their differences, feel they belong. This is vital because we have observed in our teaching that when learners feel outcast or out of place, it can be a very real barrier to learning.

For many decades, if not centuries, individuals belonging to groups that have been historically and routinely marginalized also experienced silencing and erasure. This erasure happened both passively, through a refusal to discuss institutional and interpersonal violence, and actively, through a persistent refusal to address or even talk about social norms, common language used, and other harmful practices. When we make an intentional effort to recognize heritage months and cultural celebrations, we are showing that we are ready to evolve beyond the past and to "do better now that we know better." Join us in learning about and celebrating the multiplicity of life experiences that make up this colorful woven tapestry of our world as we name and connect heritage celebrations to the themes in this guide.

Important Dates

- Back to School Month
- International Peace Month
- National Inventors Month
- American Artist Appreciation Month
- National Chocolate Chip Cookie Day (August 4)
- Book Lovers' Day (August 9)
- International Day of the World's Indigenous People (August 9)
- National Middle Child Day (August 12)
- Bon Festival (Japanese Buddhist Celebration, August 13-16)
- National Tell a Joke Day (August 16)
- National Bad Poetry Day (August 18)
- Poet's Day (August 21)
- Women's Equality Day (August 26)

Looking Ahead: September

- Hispanic Heritage Month
- International Literacy Day (September 8)

AUGUST

 SEPTEMBER

 OCTOBER

 NOVEMBER

 DECEMBER

 JANUARY

 FEBRUARY

 MARCH

 APRIL

 MAY

 JUNE

JULY

To Do

Notes

Monday	Tuesday	Wednesday
○	○	○
○	○	○
○	○	○
○	○	○
○	○	○

14

Thursday	Friday	Saturday	Sunday
○	○	○	○
○	○	○	○
○	○	○	○
○	○	○	○
○	○	○	○

Inspiration

When we feel we belong—to a group, a community, or to just one person—it fosters a sense of acceptance and inclusion that builds confidence and allows for greater vulnerability. When young people feel comfortable enough to be vulnerable, they develop the ability to be curious and engage in the act of reading to explore, expand, and understand.

The feeling of acceptance we first feel when belonging to a family unit expands as we leave home and begin to move in the world as individuals and as parts of various groups. Help build student knowledge of what it means to belong by identifying commonalities we share with those around us, as well as the things that make us different from one another. It is sometimes our differences that help us learn the most about ourselves and those around us.

Illumination

Here, you have a chance to explore belonging in your own life. Use the invitations below to engage meaningfully with this month's theme and reflect on what it means to you.

1. Where do you feel you belong?
   _____
   _____
   _____

2. What are the traits or attributes of places or people that make you feel you belong?
   _____
   _____
   _____

3. How do you feel when you feel you belong to a person or place?
   _____
   _____
   _____

4. When was the last time you felt you belonged?
   _____
   _____
   _____

5. Who makes you feel accepted or that you belong? What characteristics do these feelings of belonging have?
   _____
   _____
   _____

6. What is one thing you can do to help others feel they belong?
   _____
   _____
   _____

7. What happens when individuals don't feel they belong?
   _____
   _____
   _____

Investigation

Investigate this month's theme of belonging with your students by inviting them to complete the following activities. Think and talk about ways you can inspire belonging with your text choices.

Kindergarten to Fifth Grade

Have students choose a story from the list of recommended titles on this month's Bookshelves pages (pages 26-27) and pick one character who does or doesn't feel they belong. Then, they will write or draw the story of that character's journey toward belonging. Prompt students to answer the question, "What parts of the story show you that they belong?"

Sixth to Eighth Grade

Have students identify one character from the list of recommended titles on the Bookshelves pages (pages 26-27) and write a diary entry about their journey to belonging. Students may consider these questions.

- Does the character belong to a community or group?
- Has the character been affected by a specific event, such as the rise of Islamophobia post 9/11?
- What in their story (other characters, setting, events) made them feel a sense of belonging?

Mentor Spotlight: Jacqueline Woodson

Jacqueline Woodson is a recipient of the Coretta Scott King Author Award and was a Library of Congress National Ambassador for Young People's Literature (2018-2020) and a 2020 recipient of the MacArthur Genius Grant (2020) for her work "redefining children's and young adult literature to encompass more complex issues and reflect the lives of Black children, teenagers, and families" (MacArthur Foundation, 2020). Jacqueline Woodson is a prolific author known for her works exploring themes of belonging, identity, and self-acceptance among young people in America. Her novels often focus on the experiences of Black girls at various stages of development, highlighting their journeys to find belonging. Woodson's powerful storytelling has had a significant impact on American literature. She also served as an Ambassador Emeritus for the Every Child a Reader Organization, with a platform of Reading × Hope = Change. You can learn more about Every Child a Reader and its ambassadors on their website. Visit Jacqueline Woodson's website using the following QR code.

https://jacquelinewoodson.com

Week One

To Do

Notes

Monday

Tuesday

Wednesday

Many of the texts I read as a child have been like roadmap markers, showing me a range of life options... helping me define myself not only as a reader, but also, as a human being.

—Alfred Tatum

AUGUST

SEPTEMBER

OCTOBER

NOVEMBER

Thursday

DECEMBER

JANUARY

FEBRUARY

Friday

MARCH

APRIL

MAY

Saturday

JUNE

JULY

Sunday

19

Week Two

To Do

Notes

Monday

Tuesday

Wednesday

> Books should help us teach in ways that honor the lives, cultures, languages, and histories of every reader and writer in our classrooms.
>
> —Mariana Souto-Manning and Jessica Martell

Thursday

Friday

Saturday

Sunday

Week Three

To Do

Notes

Monday

Tuesday

Wednesday

Stories can shape how individuals and communities are perceived, and how they are respected and valued or silenced and dehumanized.

—Elizabeth Acevedo

Thursday

Friday

Saturday

Sunday

Week Four

To Do

Notes

Monday

Tuesday

Wednesday

Books provide a type of link, connecting readers with worlds they otherwise couldn't access, reminding us of ties we sometimes ignore.

—Emma Otheguy

Thursday

Friday

Saturday

Sunday

August Bookshelves

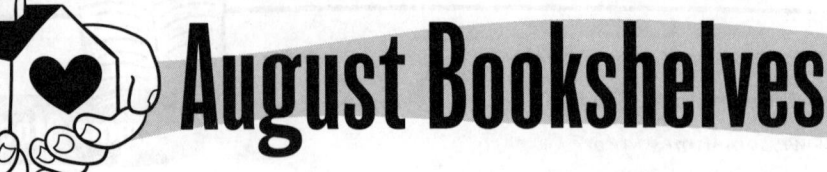

Title	Author and Illustrator	Teaching Considerations
Dictionary for a Better World: Poems, Quotes, and Anecdotes From A to Z (2020)	Irene Latham and Charles Waters, illustrated by Mehrdokht Amini	This collection of multigenre texts explores concepts related to identity, social justice, and making a difference, all of which can serve as mentor texts to inspire and imitate.
I Am Enough (2018)	Grace Byers, illustrated by Keturah A. Bobo	This wonderful model for writing with simile and metaphor is filled with poetic expressions, empowerment for girls, showing respect for diversity, and loving oneself.
I Am Every Good Thing (2020)	Derrick Barnes, illustrated by Gordon C. James	This empowering celebration of Black boys is a great model for list poems or personal narratives; it also includes a series of affirmations.
I Promise (2020)	Lebron James, illustrated by Nina Mata	This book serves as a great kickoff to building class rules and setting goals.
I Will Be Fierce (2019)	Bea Birdsong, illustrated by Nidhi Chanani	A girl finds the extraordinary in everyday moments, making this book another model for discussing or writing about affirmations.
Our Favorite Day of the Year (2020)	A. E. Ali, illustrated by Rahele Jomepour Bell	Read this book aloud to get to know more about your students, families, and their celebrations. Make a list to highlight and honor those connected to your community of learners.
Pipsqueaks, Slowpokes, and Stinkers: Celebrating Animal Underdogs (2020)	Melissa Stewart, illustrated by Stephanie Lebaris	This nonfiction text can invite conversations about finding our unique strengths and talents.

Title	Author and Illustrator	Teaching Considerations
Allies: Real Talk About Showing Up, Screwing Up, and Trying Again (2022)	Shakirah Bourne and Dana Alison Levy	This book tells real stories of allyship that individuals from diverse backgrounds have experienced, alongside examples of how those from the dominant culture have used their position, power, and privilege to help others to create a sense of belonging.
Amina's Voice (2017)	Hena Kahn	A Pakistani American Muslim girl tries to fit into her community in the U.S. amid anti-Islamic tensions. Use this text to discuss the importance of inclusion and creating communities that are welcoming and accepting even in the face of difference.
Brave (2017)	Svetlana Chmakova	This tremendously popular book is about overcoming bullies and struggles in mathematics class, along with the familiar middle school pressure to fit in.
Red, White, and Whole (2021)	Rajani LaRocca	An Indian American girl lives in a community where she is minoritized and tries to find the balance between honoring her family, their culture, and their traditions while coping with her mother's terminal illness. Use this text to teach the importance of self-discovery and acceptance even in the face of community tensions or hostility.
What Lane? (2021)	Torrey Maldonado	A biracial boy learns about racial tensions in the U. S. during the Black Lives Matter movement. He ponders the idea of staying in one's "lane," or the place society has carved out for him due to his identity. Use this text to illustrate the importance of acceptance and building community over defining others by external identity markers and socially created constructions of race.

August Bookshelves

Title	Author and Illustrator	Teaching Considerations

28

Use this blank bookshelf to reflect on books you might like to include in your teaching this month.

Title	Author and Illustrator	Teaching Considerations

Activities and Instructional Moves

Follow the invitations to help share this month's theme with your classroom. You'll find invitations and instructional guidance for elementary (K-5) and intermediate (6-8) students.

Kindergarten to Fifth Grade

- **Collect and collage inspiration:** Invite your students to gather and display inspirational quotes from books. Consider connecting the quotes to content area research conversations, too. See figure 1.1 for an example.

FIGURE 1.1: Quote box and quote collage.

- **Generate personalized inspiration:** Invite students to collect meaningful quotes and consider ways they can spread kindness like glitter. Students may also display inspirational messages on the "glitter boards" (made simply from glitter paper in a photo frame) to brighten each other's day. See figure 1.2 for an example.

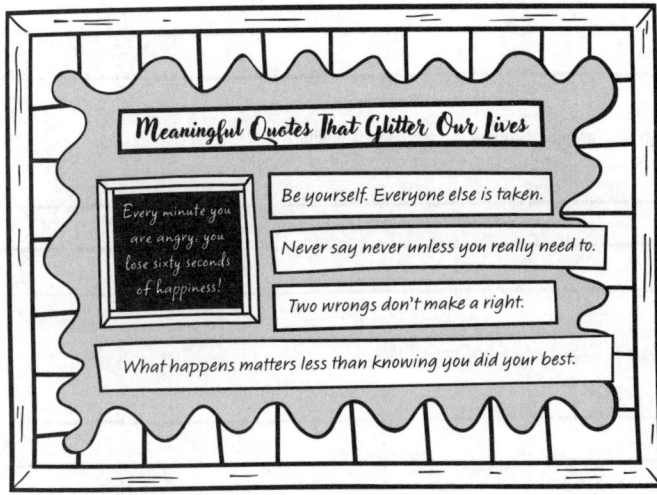

FIGURE 1.2: Glitter board.

Sixth to Eighth Grade

- **Write a multivoice poem:** Have students create a multivoice poem about a place, person, or thing they associate with belonging. A multivoice poem is usually formatted in two columns side by side and written by two or more writers. Multivoice poems often depict two perspectives of the same situation, scene, or scenario. When spoken aloud, some lines that have the same words or syntax become more impactful because there are two voices saying them. Students can use any poetic form they like, but remember, poems don't have to rhyme. Consider having students use educator Linda Christensen's (2017) book *Reading, Writing, and Rising Up* for inspiration. Then, encourage them to try reciting the poem with two or more other people.

- **Find community spaces:** Have students brainstorm to identify places in their community where people gather. What do they have in common? How are they different? Have students create an online annotated map of their community using Google Maps with notes about gathering spots and their importance.

End-of-Month Reflection Questions

1. What are some educator behaviors that help young people develop a sense of belonging?

2. What do you need to do differently in your community to help it feel more inclusive?

3. What would a young person new to your environment say about belonging?

4. Define these terms: *community*, *family*, *home*, and *acceptance*.

5. What sorts of actions by others toward you make you feel you belong?

6. What is the most important act one person can do for another to help them feel they belong?

7. What are the roles of compassion and empathy in creating communities of belonging?

SEPTEMBER

For me, joy is uninhibited, undistracted, and euphoric. It means living free to define yourself and realizing your personal and professional dreams.

—Pharrell Williams

When attempting to define the concept of joy, it can be helpful to identify what it is not. Joy isn't simply a feeling or mood that springs from nothing; in fact, "Different from mood states, joy as an emotional state is always about something, and usually, this is news about something good in one's life. Joy is a response to some good object" (Emmons, 2019). When thinking about joy as a response to a particular experience, we can transfer this understanding to the classroom, where we seek out opportunities to create joyful experiences for learners. It follows, then, that the more joy we experience as a reward for or adjacent to experiences that require effort and sometimes productive struggle, the less we will fear the latter and the more we will seek out the former.

It is so satisfying to see our students being joyful and free. Experiencing joy is like throwing a stone into a still pond; the resounding effect ripples out and touches everyone. This month, explore what it means to create space where joy is abundant and transferable via the actions we take, words we speak, and experiences we create.

Important Dates

- National Literacy Month
- Library Card Sign-Up Month
- Hispanic Heritage Month (September 15–October 15)
- World Letter Writing Day (September 1)
- National Read a Book Day (September 6)
- International Literacy Day (September 8)
- Grandparents' Day (September 10)
- National Video Games Day (September 12)
- International Dot Day (September 15)
- National Stepfamily Day (September 16)
- Read an e-Book Day (September 18)
- Native American Day (Fourth Friday of September)
- National Punctuation Day (September 24)
- Love Note Day (September 26)
- National Good Neighbor Day (September 28)
- National Love People Day (September 30)

Looking Ahead: October

- Hispanic Heritage Month (September 15–October 15)
- National Book Month
- National Information Literacy Awareness Month

SEPTEMBER

To Do

_____
_____
_____
_____
_____
_____
_____
_____

Notes

_____
_____
_____
_____
_____
_____
_____

Monday	Tuesday	Wednesday
○	○	○
○	○	○
○	○	○
○	○	○
○	○	○

Thursday	Friday	Saturday	Sunday
○	○	○	○
○	○	○	○
○	○	○	○
○	○	○	○
○	○	○	○

Inspiration

Joy is so much more than a feeling; it is a force for good and a means through which we gain energy and enthusiasm for ideas and people.

According to complex polyvagal theory, there is a specific, unique way the nervous system responds to positive external stimuli (Marter, 2023). Young people can learn to regulate the vagal nervous system by consciously listing and seeking things that bring about joy. Some refer to these positive triggers (positive external stimuli) as "glimmers." All human brains form connections between memories and experiences to create recognition and understanding. Classrooms become places where students associate joy with learning when they experience more positive connections and stimuli as a response to learning experiences.

Additionally, sharing joyful experiences in educational spaces can bring people and communities together. Think back to times when you have experienced a sudden snowfall or rainstorm together with your students, or when world events have occurred that bring individuals together in community through those shared experiences. What do you remember? What feelings have endured?

Help create classrooms filled with joy and inspire others to do the same by reading the words of teacher practitioners and writers of books for young people. Finding those who are inspired by the same things you are—serving young people and helping them become wise, curious, altruistic adults—is joyful. Teaching young people to respect and love one another through learning about differences is also one of the best things you can do to ensure learning is a pleasurable experience rather than a chore.

Illumination

Here, you have a chance to explore joy in your own life. Use the invitations below to engage meaningfully with this month's theme and reflect on what it means to you.

Complete the following phrases.

1. I feel the most joy learning something new when . . .

   _____
   _____
   _____

2. I'm most likely to experience joy in the company of . . .

   _____
   _____
   _____

3. Stories make me joyful when they are . . .

   _____
   _____
   _____

4. My last joyful experience in the classroom was . . .

   _____
   _____
   _____

Respond to the following questions.

5. When does creativity equal joy?

   _____
   _____
   _____

6. What are the qualities of an environment that is joyful?

   _____
   _____
   _____

7. What one small thing do you do each day in your classroom to inspire joy?

   _____
   _____
   _____

Investigation

Investigate this month's theme of joy with your students by inviting them to complete the following activities. Think and talk about ways you can inspire joy with your text choices.

Kindergarten to Fifth Grade

Have students choose a story from the list of recommended titles in the Bookshelves pages (pages 48-49) and one character who does or doesn't feel joy. Then, ask them to write or draw the clues that reveal they are (or are not) experiencing joy. Prompt students to answer the question, "What parts of the story make you feel joyful?"

Sixth to Eighth Grade

Have students identify one moment of joy from any of the recommended titles on the Bookshelves pages (pages 48-49). Prompt students to answer the question, "What do you think contributed to the characters in the story experiencing joy? Was it other characters, setting, events, or something else?"

Mentor Spotlight: Gholdy Muhammad

Gholdy Muhammad works with educators and students across the United States and around the world. She conducts professional development for educators on reframing mainstream education's view of Black educators and students. Her work is also structured around a pedagogy of joy, genius, and liberatory thinking through which she encourages all students (and the educators who serve them) to strive for their highest potential.

Muhammad's teaching for students and teachers focuses on the pursuit of justice and joy for all learners, especially those identifying as people of the global majority and African diaspora. Muhammad is the author of two notable books, *Cultivating Genius: An Equity Framework for Culturally and Historically Responsive Literacy* (Muhammad, 2021) and *Unearthing Joy: A Guide to Culturally and Historically Responsive Teaching and Learning* (Muhammad, 2023). Her teaching draws on cultural and historical contexts to nurture students' identity, skills, intellect, critical thinking, and joy, empowering them to learn and make a difference.

Use the following QR code to read an interview with Gholdy Muhammad.

www.edweek.org/teaching
-learning/opinion-gholdy-muhammad
-champions-unearthing-joy-in
-her-new-book/2023/02

39

Week One

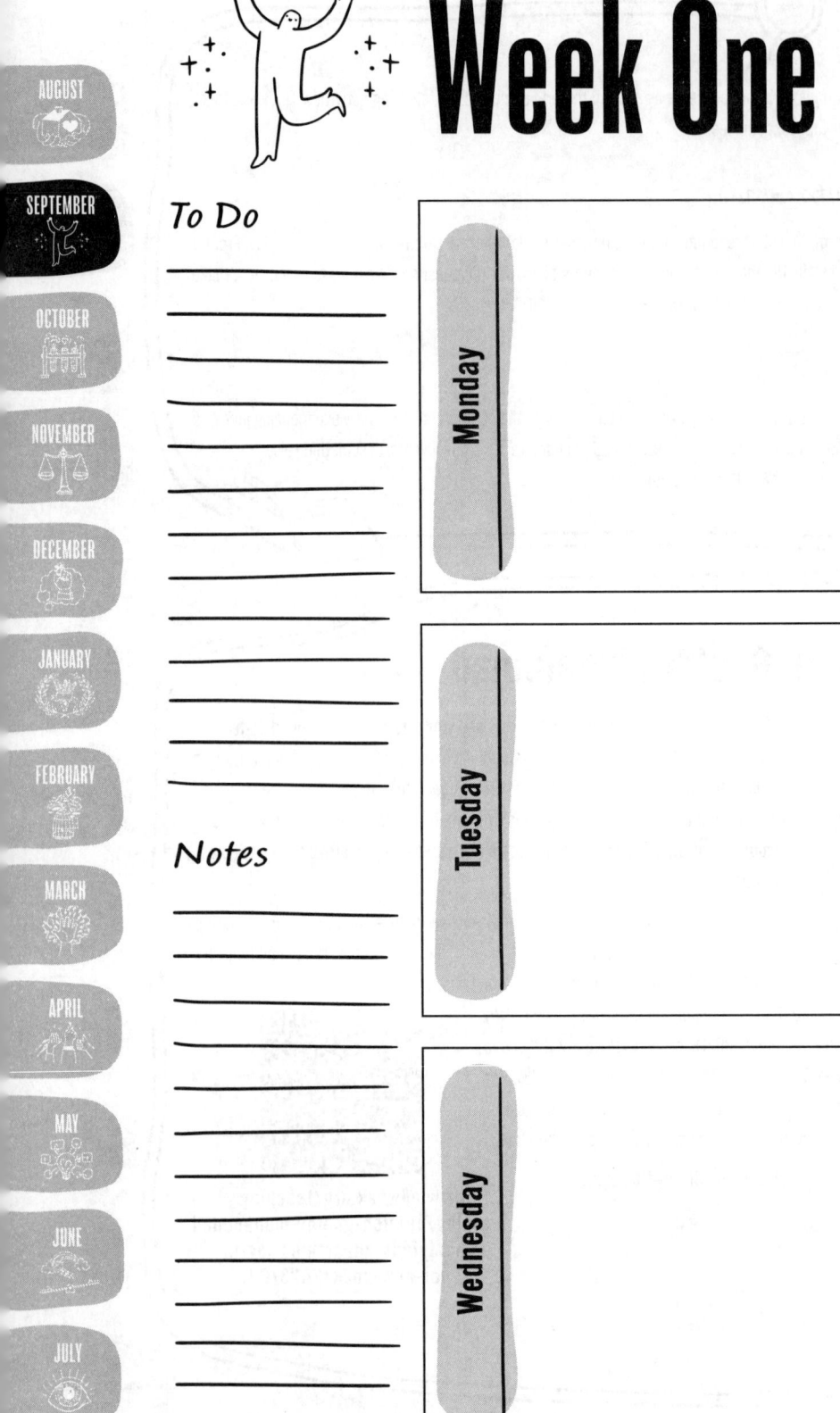

To Do

Notes

Monday

Tuesday

Wednesday

Joy is an instrumental part of making our classrooms feel like safe and jovial homes for all. With joy comes bonding, vulnerability, and communities of belonging.

—**Pam Allyn and Ernest Morrell**

Thursday

Friday

Saturday

Sunday

 AUGUST
 SEPTEMBER
 OCTOBER
 NOVEMBER
 DECEMBER
 JANUARY
 FEBRUARY
 MARCH
 APRIL
 MAY
 JUNE
 JULY

Week Two

To Do

Notes

Monday

Tuesday

Wednesday

It is our duty and our joy to communicate our hearts to each other. Words assist us in this task.

—Kate DiCamillo

Thursday

Friday

Saturday

Sunday

Week Three

To Do

Notes

Monday

Tuesday

Wednesday

We need joy as we need air. We need love as we need water. We need each other as we need the earth we share.

—Maya Angelou

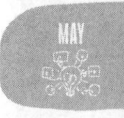

Thursday

Friday

Saturday

Sunday

Week Four

To Do

Notes

Monday

Tuesday

Wednesday

Make joy a learning goal.

—Gholdy Muhammad

Thursday

Friday

Saturday

Sunday

September Bookshelves

Title	Author and Illustrator	Teaching Considerations
A Is for All the Things You Are: A Joyful ABC Book (2019)	Anna Forgerson Hindley, illustrated by Keturah A. Bobo	Affirming adjectives in this book celebrate what makes us unique and connects us. Consider creating your own alliterative alphabet book (names and concepts connected to joy or another theme).
All My Treasures: A Book of Joy (2016)	Jo Witek, illustrated by Christine Roussey	This book explores the array of tangible and intangible things that can bring one joy. Students can discuss or write about their "treasures."
A House for Every Bird (2021)	Megan Maynor, illustrated by Kaylani Juanita	This powerful text has layers of meaning and teaches about the harms of making assumptions. Use this book as a tool to ask questions, honor student voices, and find joy in all that makes us unique individuals.
Layla's Happiness (2019)	Mariahadessa Ekere Tallie, illustrated by Ashleigh Corrin	This book invites conversations about what brings people joy. When reading, suggest students pair up to discuss, draw, or make notes in their writers' notebooks.
My Very Favorite Book in the Whole Wide World (2021)	Malcolm Mitchell, illustrated by Michael Robertson	As you get to know your students, this book invites questions to share what they know, love, and care about. Start a personal or class favorite list of books and authors.
Read! Read! Read! (2017)	Amy Ludwig VanDerwater, illustrated by Ryan O'Rourke	Also check out its companion, *Write! Write! Write!* (2020). This collection of poems celebrates the act of reading, from the initial triumphant moment of decoding words to the lifelong pleasure of getting lost in a good book. The enthusiasm in these poems is contagious and can inspire young readers.

Title	Author and Illustrator	Teaching Considerations
Barakah Beats (2022)	Maleeha Siddiqui	A young girl joins an all-boy band to fit in, even though music isn't allowed in Islam. Use this text to explore how music and the arts can bring joy and liberation to individuals and communities.
Ghost (2017)	Jason Reynolds	A young, naturally talented athlete and troublemaker finds out who he can count on as he discovers his gift. Use this text to teach about the confidence that comes from discovering one's gifts and the joy found in family and community.
A High Five for Glenn Burke (2021)	Phil Bildner	This moving work of LGBTQIA historical fiction tells about coming out and inviting others in. Use this text to discuss the importance of recognizing and respecting identities as a source of joy.
Operation Sisterhood (2022)	Olugbemisola Rhuday-Perkovich	This character-driven story tells about a young girl finding her way in a new blended family. Use this book to discuss family, friends, and found family as sources of joy.
Rez Dogs (2022)	Joseph Bruchac	A young Wabanaki girl befriends a local dog and learns about her ancestors. Use this text to explore the importance of friendship and intergenerational connections as sources of joy.
Stand Up, Yumi Chung! (2020)	Jessica Kim	A young Asian American girl becomes a comedian when she is mistaken for another student at a kids' comedy camp. Use this story to discuss the importance of laughter and cultural and individual perceptions that determine whether something is humorous.
Ways to Make Sunshine (2021)	Renée Watson	A little girl in Portland, Oregon tries to find ways to bring sunshine into the lives of her loved ones. Use this novel to teach the importance of being a source of joy in the lives of others and the impact this can have on communities and society as a whole.

September Bookshelves

Title	Author and Illustrator	Teaching Considerations

Use this blank bookshelf to reflect on books you might like to include in your teaching this month.

Title	Author and Illustrator	Teaching Considerations

Activities and Instructional Moves

Follow the invitations to help share this month's theme with your classroom. You'll find invitations and instructional guidance for elementary (K–5) and intermediate (6–8) students.

Kindergarten to Fifth Grade

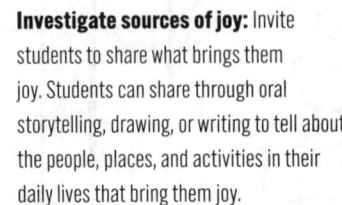

- **Investigate sources of joy:** Invite students to share what brings them joy. Students can share through oral storytelling, drawing, or writing to tell about the people, places, and activities in their daily lives that bring them joy.

- **Celebrate joy at home:** Consider connecting the conversation about joy to your students' lives both at home and at school. What do students like to read or write about that brings them joy? Where do they feel the most joyful at play, at rest, or when working?

Sixth to Eighth Grade

- **Write found poems:** Have students create found poems exploring the concept of joy by taking snippets of already existing text and combining them into new poems; visit www.poets.org/glossary/found-poem for more details. Present poets such as Shel Silverstein and Margarita Engle as models.

- **Write shape poems:** Have students write poems in the shape of an object that brings joy. Give them an emotions wheel (feelingswheel.com, for instance) if they feel they need other words for joy.

- **Create a gallery walk:** Share joy with others in your community by having students make an interactive gallery walk of joyful people, places, events, or ideas. Consider including QR codes that link to online content.

- **Enjoy Middle Ground Book Fest:** This is a virtual middle grade book festival for educators, librarians, writers, and readers. Use their YouTube channel (www.youtube.com/c/MiddleGroundBookFest) to generate excitement about new titles or encourage students to explore and create themed vlogs of their own (using those on the site as models) around themes such as crushes, brave girl characters, or anything else that sparks their imaginations.

End-of-Month Reflection Questions

1. What types of experiences create feelings of joy?

   _____
   _____
   _____

2. How can educational spaces help young people connect joy with learning?

   _____
   _____
   _____

3. Is it possible to experience discomfort and joy at the same time?

   _____
   _____
   _____

4. What are some characteristics of people who bring joy?

   _____
   _____
   _____

5. What connections can you make between joy and memory?

   _____
   _____
   _____

6. How can we reward students for creating joyful experiences for themselves and others?

   _____
   _____
   _____

7. What correlations can you find between curiosity, exploration, and joy?

   _____
   _____
   _____

OCTOBER

Inquiry

Education is not about sitting and listening, it's about being able to run with the new ideas.

—**Mae Jemison**

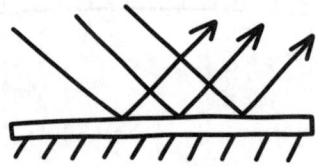

When we say we are grounded in inquiry-based learning, it is really a call to our higher selves.

According to research, in inquiry-based learning, students act like scientists, using similar methods and practices to construct knowledge (Keselman, 2003). Inquiry-based learning can be further defined as a "process of discovering new causal relations, with the learner formulating hypotheses and testing them by conducting experiments and/or making observations" (Pedaste, Mäeots, Leijen, & Sarapuu, 2012).

This higher self yearns for answers to life's biggest questions. All students begin their journeys in life by learning about the world with curiosity. They start by understanding their families, caregivers, and immediate surroundings. Then, they gradually expand outward into the neighborhood, community, and geographic region. Eventually, we hope to encourage students to explore the world and ask questions about it that may lead to identifying answers—if not solutions—to some of humanity's age-old questions. Guide students through a journey of discovery with the text sets and questions this month. See what questions arise for them and for you. Rediscover the young person in you as you learn alongside them.

Important Dates

- Learning Disabilities Awareness Month
- National Book Mont
- TeenTober™ (the American Library Association [2023] describes TeenTober as "a nationwide celebration hosted by libraries every October [that] aims to celebrate teens, promote year-round teen services and the innovative ways teen services helps teens learn new skills, and fuel their passions in and outside the library.")
- National Economic Education Month
- Fire Prevention Month
- Attention-Deficit / Hyperactivity Disorder Awareness Month
- National Principals Month
- Banned Books Week (Banned Books Week is sometimes, but not always, recognized by the American Library Association [ALA] as the last week of September.)
- National Friends of Libraries Week
- National Hair Day (October 1)
- National Custodian Recognition Day (October 2)
- Random Acts of Poetry Day (first Wednesday of October)
- World Smile Day (first Friday of October)
- World Teachers' Day (October 5
- Black Poetry Day (October 17)
- National Day on Writing (October 20)

Looking Ahead: November

- National Native American Heritage Month
- National Family Literacy Month

OCTOBER

To Do

Notes

Monday	Tuesday	Wednesday
○	○	○
○	○	○
○	○	○
○	○	○
○	○	○

Thursday	Friday	Saturday	Sunday
◯	◯	◯	◯
◯	◯	◯	◯
◯	◯	◯	◯
◯	◯	◯	◯
◯	◯	◯	◯

Inspiration

We regard inquiry-based learning as a natural, historical evolution from the earliest days of Socrates and Confucius, when teachers and students learned by going back and forth asking one another increasingly profound questions about whatever subject was at hand (Peters, 2014). In today's educational landscape, inquiry-based learning centers on student curiosity and interests. It is more about the experience and the journey than the outcome and a finished product. Remembering that it is the journey that often teaches us more than the destination allows us to think differently about inquiry.

Gather inspiration for your inquiry-based instruction directly from your students. Ask them questions that will lead to more questions. An idea frequently attributed to Paulo Freire is "remember the magic that happens when the teacher becomes the student and the student becomes the teacher."

Illumination

Here, you have a chance to explore inquiry in your own life. Use the invitations below to engage meaningfully with this month's theme and reflect on what it means to you.

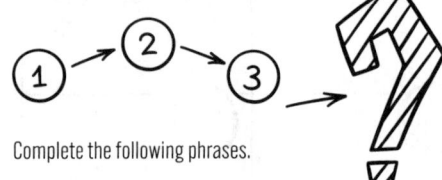

Complete the following phrases.

1. I become most curious when . . .

2. When I'm curious, I usually take these steps . . .

3. The best stories are those that leave . . . to the reader.

Respond to the following questions.

4. When inquiry-based instruction works, it is . . .

5. Does a question always have to have a clear answer? Why or why not?

6. What are the qualities of a good inquiry-based lesson?

7. What, other than natural curiosity, inspires inquiry?

Investigation

Investigate this month's theme of inquiry with your students by inviting them to complete the following activities. Think and talk about ways you can inspire inquiry with your text choices.

Kindergarten to Fifth Grade

Have students choose a story from the list of recommended titles in this month's Bookshelves pages (pages 70-71) and ask them to consider the way it may have made them change their view or think about something in a new way. In addition, students may consider the way the character or content was driven by a passion to wonder. Add your own new wonderings, too, and share them with students.

Sixth to Eighth Grade

Have students identify one moment of inquiry that came from reading any of the titles in this month's Bookshelves pages (pages 70-71). Prompt students to answer the question, "What do you think contributed to the characters in the story finding answers to their questions? Were they affected by other characters, setting, events, or something else?"

Mentor Spotlight: Melissa Stewart

Melissa Stewart is a prolific author of over 200 informational books for young readers. Her work covers a wide range of topics, including animals, technology, and physical science. Many educators utilize her books as mentor texts in their classrooms. Stewart's website offers a wealth of resources for students and educators alike, including materials designed to inspire reading, writing, and critical thinking.

Stewart's nonfiction resources include the 2020 book *Nonfiction Writers Dig Deep: 50 Award-Winning Authors Share the Secret of Engaging Writing* and, coauthored with Marlene Correia (2023), *5 Kinds of Nonfiction: Enriching Reading and Writing Instruction With Children's Books*. These books expose readers to an array of titles and authors to inspire inquiry and offer support for reading and writing about informative topics. With Nancy Chesley, Stewart (2014, 2016) coauthored *Perfect Pairs: Using Fiction & Nonfiction Picture Books to Teach Life Science, K-2* and the companion volume for grades 3-5 students; both books connect picture books to science standards.

Visit Melissa Stewart's website using the following QR code.

https://melissa-stewart.com

Week One

To Do

Notes

Monday

Tuesday

Wednesday

> *One of our main jobs as educators is to connect kids to curiosities they didn't even know they had.*
>
> —Kristin Ziemke

Thursday

Friday

Saturday

Sunday

Week Two

To Do

Notes

Monday

Tuesday

Wednesday

One of the goals of education is not simply to fill students with facts and information but to help them learn how to learn.

—Zaretta L. Hammond

AUGUST

SEPTEMBER

OCTOBER

Thursday

NOVEMBER

DECEMBER

Friday

JANUARY

FEBRUARY

MARCH

Saturday

APRIL

MAY

JUNE

Sunday

JULY

Week Three

To Do

Notes

Monday

Tuesday

Wednesday

Research is formalized curiosity. It is poking and prying with a purpose.

—**Zora Neale Hurston**

Thursday

Friday

Saturday

Sunday

Week Four

To Do

Notes

Monday

Tuesday

Wednesday

Education as inquiry suggests that the personal and collective questions of learners ought to be the heart of curriculum.

—Jerome C. Harste

Thursday

Friday

Saturday

Sunday

69

October Bookshelves

Title	Author and Illustrator	Teaching Considerations
Butt or Face? (2023)	Kari Lavelle	This engaging nonfiction book will have readers laughing and learning. Share to discuss widening perspectives and explore further investigations.
Friends Beyond Measure (2023)	Lalena Fisher	This friendship story is told through various charts. Its layout will invite opportunities to dig deeper into infographics and may encourage further investigations.
Out of Wonder: Celebrating Poets and Poetry (2021)	Kwame Alexander and Eukea Holmes	The poetic tributes in this book invite readers to wonder, learn, and write their own poetry.
Wish in a Tree (2025)	Lynda Mullaly Hunt, illustrated by Nancy Carpenter	This picture book complements Hunt's novel *Fish in a Tree*, which won the Schneider Family Book Award in 2016. Share this story to honor neurodiversity, curiosity, and inquiry and as a way to invite conversations about the many ways we are smart, different, and unique.
A Walk in the Words (2021)	Hudson Talbott	In honor of Learning Disabilities Awareness Month, this book reflects the author's own experiences learning to read. Share to reflect on our literacy journeys and plan goals to grow.
Wonder Walkers (2021)	Micha Archer	With thought-provoking questions, this story centers on curious kids and the power of wondering about ourselves, others, and our world.

Title	Author and Illustrator	Teaching Considerations
Everything You Wanted to Know About Indians but Were Afraid to Ask: Young Readers Edition (2021)	Anton Treuer	Explore questions about Native Americans with cultural preservationist and scholar Anton Treuer. Use this text to explore questions about cultures and people who may be new to your community and learn how you can respectfully recognize differences and similarities.
The Jumbies (2015)	Tracey Baptiste	Mixing the supernatural and Caribbean folklore traditions, Baptiste weaves a tale about a spirited young heroine who uses her gifts to solve real-world issues. Use this novel to teach curiosity and discovery rather than suspicion and mistrust when presented with "outsiders" or identities that are new.
The Parker Inheritance (2018)	Varian Johnson	Tweenaged friends set out to find an inheritance, and along the way, wind up investigating how to exonerate a family member and expose an injustice once committed against an African American family. Use this novel to teach about the importance of uncovering complete histories of individuals and communities.
StarTalk: Everything You Ever Need To Know About Space Travel, Sci-Fi, the Human Race, the Universe, and Beyond (2016)	Neil deGrasse Tyson	Uncover the mysteries of space, science, and the universe as well as amusing questions like the likelihood of a zombie apocalypse. Use this text to explore big questions young readers have always wanted the answers to.
The Vanquishers (2023)	Kalynn Bayron	Tweenaged vampire hunters try to find their missing friend in a supernatural mystery involving teamwork and investigation. Use this text to teach about mystery and the supernatural, how we investigate fact from fiction, and the roots of superstition.

October Bookshelves

Title	Author and Illustrator	Teaching Considerations

Use this blank bookshelf to reflect on books you might like to include in your teaching this month.

Title	Author and Illustrator	Teaching Considerations

Activities and Instuctional Moves

Follow the invitations to help share this month's theme with your classroom. You'll find invitations and instructional guidance for elementary (K-5) and intermediate (6-8) students.

Kindergarten to Fifth Grade

- **Conduct wonder-full investigations:** Provide time and space for students to brainstorm about things they wonder or want to know more about. Invite students to keep track using a "wonder wall" bulletin board in the classroom or with digital tools such as Padlet. Students can also draw or write about things they would like to investigate. This activity is similar to Georgia Heard's heart maps (www.georgiaheard.com/heart-maps) and Nancie Atwell's (2002) writing territories but invites learners to consider their passions as they plan to read, write, and investigate their world. See figure 3.1 for an example.

- **Conduct inquiry studies (find words, facts, and ideas that make you say "wow"):** Invite inquiry and investigation into all aspects of your day. Read informational texts often. Curate a collection of texts in your school or classroom library that will serve as sources of investigation. Suggest that your students gather books on a topic that they would like to explore further. You may also want to consider revisiting the many ways of taking notes and locating things that make them go "*wow*." As applicable, focus on charts your students could use to share the information they have learned. See figure 3.2 for an example.

FIGURE 3.1: Sample wonder wall.

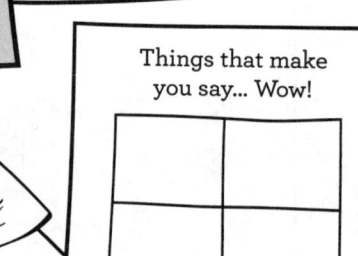

FIGURE 3.2: Things that make you say "wow" template.

*Visit **go.SolutionTree.com/literacy** for a free reproducible version of this figure.*

Sixth to Eighth Grade

- **Pursue a mystery:** Using the resources available to them, have students investigate mysteries in their community, such as unsolved cases or haunted houses. Then, combine the mysteries and create a museum crawl (a series of mini posters, presentations on laptops, or QR codes) with information about each mystery and classroom theories as to what really happened.

- **Design a Museum of the Future exhibit:** Have students choose an individual or event from history and complete an inquiry chart that helps them process what they think they know about a subject, what they learn during their visit that challenges or confirms what they knew, what they can dispel as a misconception, and, finally, any new questions they may have. Ask them to create a multimedia presentation about their topic for the class Museum of the Future so that people in the future can learn about the past from different perspectives. Consider helping students create a virtual room with clickable objects that hyperlink to more information. Often, the official website of a museum or historical center will feature a virtual tour of their space. George Washington's home Mount Vernon (www.mountvernon.org), for example, includes an interactive tour of the venue with many interesting anecdotes attached. See figure 3.3 for a sample inquiry chart, inspired by Tony Stead's (2014) chart to Read and Analyze Nonfiction (RAN).

What We Think We Know	Yes, We Were Right (Confirmed Info)	Misconceptions	What New Things We Have Learned	What New Questions We Have

FIGURE 3.3: Inquiry chart.

*Visit **go.SolutionTree.com/literacy** for a free reproducible version of this figure.*

End-of-Month Reflection Questions

1. What types of places and people spark your curiosity?
   _____
   _____
   _____

2. What would you like to investigate or explore if you had infinite time and resources?
   _____
   _____
   _____

3. Who are you the most curious about (from history or the present)?
   _____
   _____
   _____

4. What do you think humans of the future will think about our time?
   _____
   _____
   _____

5. What resources do you need to get answers to big unanswered questions?
   _____
   _____
   _____

6. Why do you think some of the world's greatest mysteries remain unsolved (for example, how exactly the Egyptian pyramids were constructed)?
   _____
   _____
   _____

7. What information do you need to prove something is true or real?
   _____
   _____
   _____

NOVEMBER

Justice

One child, one teacher, one book, one pen can change the world.

—**Malala Yousafzai**

When we think about justice, our minds often go to great people who have fought for justice on behalf of others: Mahatma Ghandi, Benazir Bhutto, Nelson Mandela, Dr. Martin Luther King Jr., Deb Haaland, and even Bob Marley, to name just a few. Each of these individuals began as a student in school. Each of them was inspired to work toward justice using their unique gifts and talents as they were nurtured (or tried and tested) in various ways.

An elementary concept of justice is that individuals should be treated fairly and equally, receiving what they deserve based on their actions, pertaining to punishments or rewards. In literature, we often elevate authors who write about the pursuit of justice or events (real or imagined) in which justice has been hard won. In this way, we teach young readers both about the pursuit of justice as it evolves with every generation and that the circumstances that bring about injustice are always influenced by social and cultural contexts.

We believe in the mantra "Always be mentored, always be mentoring," and so we see that the unbreakable chain between mentor dedicated to justice and mentee inspired to move toward justice continues throughout time. This month, think about those who have inspired your understanding of what justice really means and what it might take to inspire the young people in your community to strive for justice, even when it seems the odds are stacked against them.

Important Dates

- National Native American Heritage Month
- Puerto Rican Heritage Month
- National Picture Book Month
- National Family Literacy Month
- National Book Awards
- National Young Readers Week (second week of November)
- American Education Week (third week of November)
- National Hunger and Homelessness Awareness Week (the week before Thanksgiving)
- National Family Literacy Day and National Author's Day (November 1)
- National STEAM (science, technology, engineering, art, and math) Day (November 8)
- Veterans Day (November 11)
- School Psychologist Week (November 11-15)
- Education Support Professional Day (the Wednesday of American Education Week)
- World Kindness Day (November 13)
- National Listening Day (Friday after Thanksgiving Day)

Looking Ahead: December

- National Month of Universal Human Rights
- National Short Story Day (December 21)
- Yule Book Flood Day (December 24)

NOVEMBER

To Do

Notes

Monday	Tuesday	Wednesday
○	○	○
○	○	○
○	○	○
○	○	○
○	○	○

Thursday	Friday	Saturday	Sunday
○	○	○	○
○	○	○	○
○	○	○	○
○	○	○	○
○	○	○	○

Inspiration

Who or what are some of the individuals or movements that have informed your ideas of justice? Some of the ways we form an understanding of big concepts like justice are when we experience the absence of them (injustice) or when we have a deep-seated feeling that something just isn't right. It is instinctive to move toward situations and people who bring about equality and away from those who do not. However, there have been plenty of times throughout history when movements that were deeply rooted in injustice caught fire and gained the following of many.

Consider book banning, which happens in many nations across the globe and, in some societies, has always existed. For example, one of the first book bannings in the United States took place in Quincy, Massachusetts in 1637, when the Puritan government banned Thomas Morton's *New English Canaan* because it was a "harsh and heretical critique of Puritan customs and power structures" (Gutman Library, 2024). Since that time, book challenges, in which a community or group of people campaigned against a book's inclusion in a library collection or classroom curriculum, have come and gone with each new interpretation of the First Amendment. The reasons books are banned is cyclical in nature. Some stories do not have correct or affirming representations and others do not include representation of marginalized groups or individuals at all. This leads to ignorance or lack of familiarity with lived realities and experiences beyond a very limited scope. From ignorance and lack of understanding comes fear, and from there the censorship cycle gets and gains traction.

For more information and support to respond to book challenges, the following resources are available online.

- **American Library Association's Library Bill of Rights** (www.ala.org/advocacy/intfreedom/librarybill): This page outlines the ALA's Library Bill of Rights, which provides principles on intellectual freedom and access to information, advocating for libraries to offer resources without censorship or restriction.

- **ALA Office for Intellectual Freedom** (www.ala.org/aboutala/offices/oif): The Office for Intellectual Freedom protects the rights of library users by offering resources, advocacy, and support related to issues of censorship, privacy, and the freedom to read.

- **National Council of Teachers of English (NCTE) Intellectual Freedom Center** (www.ncte.org/resources/ncte-intellectual-freedom-center): This center provides resources and support to educators facing censorship challenges and offers tools for defending students' rights to access diverse and inclusive texts.

- **Texas FReadom Fighters** (www.txfreadomfighters.us): This page highlights the work of a group of Texas librarians committed to protecting intellectual freedom, uplifting the work of teachers and librarians, and providing professional resources to support those facing book challenges.

Illumination

Here, you have a chance to explore justice in your own life. Use the invitations below to engage meaningfully with this month's theme and reflect on what it means to you.

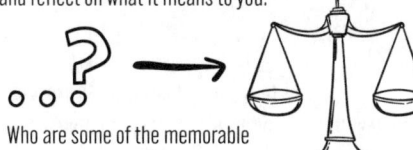

1. Who are some of the memorable people in the pursuit of justice?

   _____
   _____
   _____

2. Nineteenth-century abolitionist and Unitarian minister Theodore Parker (1853) once said, "I do not pretend to understand the moral universe; the arc is a long one . . . And from what I see I am sure it bends toward justice" (p. 84). This quote was popularized later by Martin Luther King Jr., who used it in many of his speeches. Do you agree with this sentiment? Why or why not?

   _____
   _____
   _____

3. What makes someone passionate about the pursuit of justice?

   _____
   _____
   _____

4. What makes a person move from standing by to taking action?

   _____
   _____
   _____

5. What would you consider to be some of the most successful movements in the pursuit of justice?

   _____
   _____
   _____

6. What types of justice interest you the most (such as climate justice, LGBTQIA equality, or others)?

   _____
   _____
   _____

7. Do you think the world is a more just place overall than it was a hundred years ago? Why or why not?

   _____
   _____
   _____

Investigation

Investigate this month's theme of justice with your students by inviting them to complete the following activities. Think and talk about ways you can inspire justice with your text choices.

Kindergarten to Fifth Grade

How can stories help evoke thoughts, feelings, and questions as well as teach students to raise their voices and take action? Invite your learners to revisit a story, event, or character from this month's Bookshelves titles (pages 94-95). Encourage your students to discuss their connections to those experiences. How might they be the same, how might they be different, and why? In what ways might your students use their voices to create change in your community?

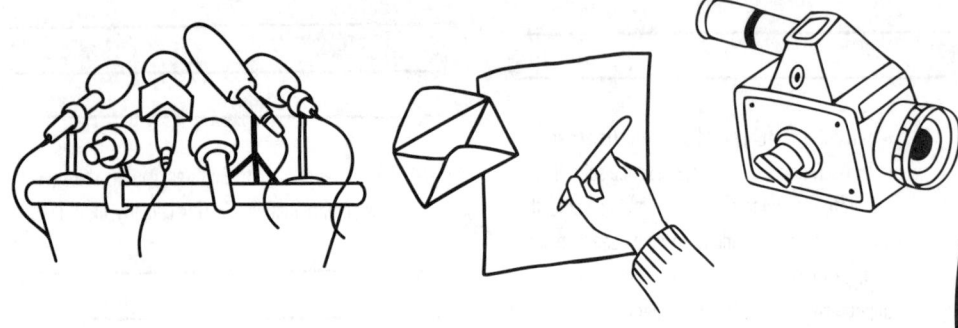

Sixth to Eighth Grade

Have students identify one or more moments in any of the suggested titles where individuals worked toward the pursuit of justice. Prompt them to answer the following questions.

- What were some of the character traits they developed?
- What were some of the challenges they faced along the way?
- How did they overcome them?

Then, ask students to consider what is necessary to pursue justice and when individuals or institutions will know they have achieved it.

Think and talk about ways you can develop an awareness of the reasons for and outcomes of pursuing justice through your text choices.

Mentor Spotlight: Miranda Paul

Miranda Paul is an award-winning author and activist whose books often explore environmental themes and encourage readers to take action. She is a co-founder of We Need Diverse Books, an organization advocating for greater diversity and representation in children's literature. Paul actively engages with schools and provides extensive resources for educators and families on her website. These resources include teacher guides for her books, which offer cross-curricular connections to subjects like literacy, science, math, art, and social studies. She also provides activity ideas, project suggestions, and behind-the-scenes interviews to further enrich the reading experience.

Visit Miranda Paul's website using the following QR code.

https://mirandapaul.com

Week One

To Do

Notes

Monday

Tuesday

Wednesday

If we want a beloved community, we must stand for justice.

—bell hooks

Thursday

Friday

Saturday

Sunday

Week Two

To Do

Notes

Monday

Tuesday

Wednesday

Never forget that justice is what love looks like in public.

—Cornel West

Thursday

Friday

Saturday

Sunday

AUGUST
SEPTEMBER
OCTOBER
NOVEMBER
DECEMBER
JANUARY
FEBRUARY
MARCH
APRIL
MAY
JUNE
JULY

Week Three

To Do

Notes

Monday

Tuesday

Wednesday

Injustice anywhere is a threat to justice everywhere.

—Martin Luther King Jr.

Thursday

Friday

Saturday

Sunday

Week Four

To Do

Notes

Monday

Tuesday

Wednesday

All acts of kindness are lights in the war for justice.

—Joy Harjo

Thursday

Friday

Saturday

Sunday

November Bookshelves

Title	Author and Illustrator	Teaching Considerations
An American Story (2023)	Kwame Alexander, illustrated by Dare Coulter	This powerful picture book can help teach about slavery and other aspects of history through the lens of hope. Encourage your students to keep notes as they read and investigate multiple perspectives.
Beautiful Hands (2015)	Kathryn Otoshi and Bret Baumgarten	Share this text and its surprising images to celebrate all the wonderful things that one's hands, hearts, and minds can do. Consider creating a mural or art project inspired by these handprints and other ideas.
Change Sings: A Children's Anthem (2021)	Amanda Gorman, illustrated by Loren Long	Presidential inaugural poet and activist Amanda Gorman created an anthem to empower all readers to be the change they wish to see in the world. What might your students want to change?
Thank You, Omu! (2018)	Oge Mora	This book is a celebration of community, giving, and gratitude. Make a list of community members you and your students are grateful for.
Thanku: Poems of Gratitude (2019)	Miranda Paul, illustrated by Marlena Myles	This collection of poetry explores ways to find gratitude every day. Invite your students to write thank you notes or poems to express their gratitude to special people in their lives.
We Are Still Here! Native American Truths Everyone Should Know (2021)	Traci Sorell, illustrated by Frané Lessac	This picture book is a wonderful addition to classroom collections to honor Native Americans. Invite your students to investigate their impact on various traditions, past and present.

94

Title	Author and Illustrator	Teaching Considerations
Born Behind Bars (2023)	Padma Venkatraman	This novel, based on actual events, tells the tale of a young person born in prison and then learning to adjust to life on the outside. Use this text to teach about those who are imprisoned for crimes they did not commit.
From the Desk of Zoe Washington (2021)	Janae Marks	In this novel, labeled "realistic fiction," a young girl learns to use activism to fight against injustice. Use this novel to teach about the injustices within the American justice system.
Just Mercy: A True Story of the Fight for Justice (Adapted for Young Adults; 2019)	Bryan Stevenson	This autobiographical tale is about the founder of the Equal Justice Initiative. Use it to teach how young people become activists and how systems of justice can become corrupt if not understood and defended.
My Family Divided: One Girl's Journey of Home, Loss, and Hope (2019)	Diane Guerrero and Erica Moroz	This autobiographical tale tells the story of undocumented immigrants and broken families. Use it to discuss foreign policy and immigration as well as the reasons individuals choose to migrate or become refugees.
They Called Us Enemy (2019)	George Takei, Justin Eisinger, and Steven Scott, illustrated by Harmony Becker	This graphic novel tells an autobiographical story of Japanese American internment. Use it to teach about injustices committed against entire groups of people who are othered and marginalized by the communities they help to build.

November Bookshelves

Title	Author and Illustrator	Teaching Considerations

Use this blank bookshelf to reflect on books you might like to include in your teaching this month.

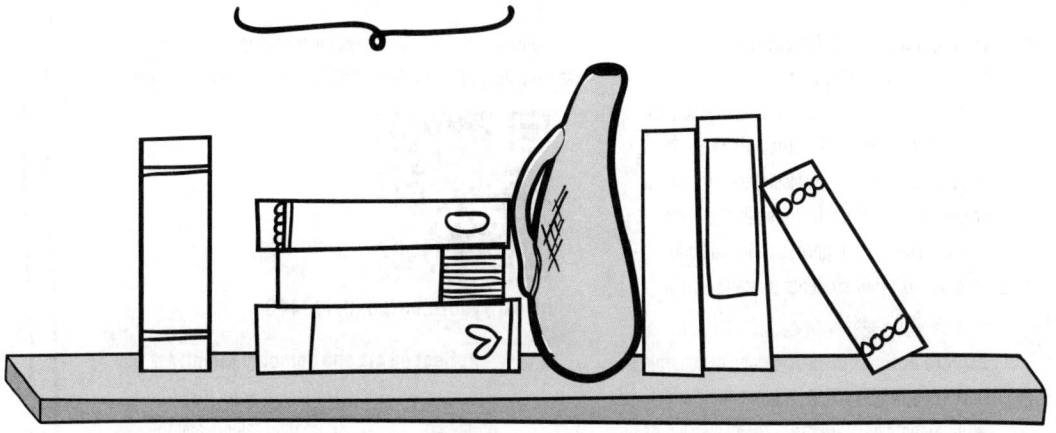

Title	Author and Illustrator	Teaching Considerations

Activities and Instructional Moves

Follow the invitations to help share this month's theme with your classroom. You'll find invitations and instructional guidance for elementary (K-5) and intermediate (6-8) students.

Kindergarten to Fifth Grade

- **Find opportunities for service:** It's important to always stand up for what is right and just. Invite your students to consider issues in your school or community that they would like to impact. Students may seek support from local organizations and might consider starting a food or book drive or perhaps a lunch buddy program. Ask your students to brainstorm a list of possibilities.

- **Explore activist identity:** Consider sharing Nikkolas Smith's (2023) picture book *The Artivist* with students or share the author's own words on what it means to be an artist and an activist. Discuss these ideas with your students. You may also pose the following questions.
    - What social justice movements do you most admire?
    - In what ways could you have a positive influence in this world?
    - How does *The Artivist* inspire you to use your art and creativity to do so?

Consider showing your class the following YouTube video, written and illustrated by Smith (2024), about being an artivist.

https://youtu.be/L0k0xIY044Q

- **Reflect on art and personal talent:** Ask your students to reflect on ways they could share their talents and the various forms of art, such as film, dance, poetry, and more, to inspire others and make a positive change. Smith's (2023) beautiful work serves as a call to action for healing, equity, and inclusion.

Sixth to Eighth Grade

- **Create a social media campaign:** Have students develop a social media campaign or short documentary about an issue of their choice. Remind them to include the problem, causes, and possible solutions with a call to action at the end.

- **Investigate issues mentioned in books:** Tell students to consider the various books they have read or previewed during this month that focused on justice. Have them investigate one of the issues discussed (Japanese American internment, false imprisonment, and so on) or another issue of their choice. Together, create a wall of remembrance in your school library or other community space for people to learn more about individuals impacted by injustice.

End-of-Month Reflection Questions

1. What movements for justice do you most admire?

   _____
   _____
   _____

2. Who do you think has been the most successful in their pursuit of justice and what tactics did they use to achieve their goals?

   _____
   _____
   _____

3. What do you think future leaders should consider about the pursuit of justice?

   _____
   _____
   _____

4. What resources do individuals need to be successful in the pursuit of justice?

   _____
   _____
   _____

5. Why do you think some movements succeed and others fail?

   _____
   _____
   _____

6. Why do you think it takes so long in some cases to achieve equality and justice?

   _____
   _____
   _____

DECEMBER

Remembrance

Memories of our lives, of our works, and our deeds will continue in others.

—**Rosa Parks**

What do you know about the connection between memory and creating a shared history? When considering literature, our memories of favorite stories connect us to one another and to a collective memory. Regarding nonfiction, memory of the past is what creates a shared history for individuals, communities, nations, and humanity. Literacy instruction is a vehicle for creating a shared understanding of the past and a way for us as individuals to leave a record of the past and the present for future generations.

As you look through this month, consider what you remember of your history, what has remained, and what might have been lost to time. The texts and activities in this section are designed to help you and your students consider the importance of documenting the present for the future and analyzing the past with a critical lens to understand a complete picture of what has come before.

Important Dates

- National Special Education Day (December 2)
- Take Your Child to a Bookstore Day (first Saturday of December)
- National Letter Writing Day (December 7)
- Human Rights Day (December 10)
- National App Day (December 11)
- National Short Story Day (December 21)
- Winter Solstice (December 21, 22, or 23)
- Yule Book Flood Day (December 24)
- National Thank You Note Day (December 26)

Looking Ahead: January

- National Month of Creativity
- National Book Blitz Month
- ALA Youth Media Award Celebrations (third Monday of January)
- National Braille Literacy Month

DECEMBER

To Do

Notes

Monday	Tuesday	Wednesday
○	○	○
○	○	○
○	○	○
○	○	○
○	○	○

Thursday	Friday	Saturday	Sunday
○	○	○	○
○	○	○	○
○	○	○	○
○	○	○	○
○	○	○	○

Inspiration

An uncredited but popular aphorism states, "History is told by the victors." However, in librarianship, it is known that those who preserve and organize information (texts, media, and other records of human creation) determine access and how long stories remain in the collective memory. In literacy education, certain stories have remained prevalent in the canon and are taught over and over again. With nonfiction, the stories of certain individuals are lifted up while others remain hidden. This tendency to elevate some stories while allowing others to remain buried is the window through which we can see our bias and preference for some privileged individuals and members of society and the exclusion of others. However, it is never too late to make a change. Educator and scholar Cody Miller (2018) mentions in his NCTE blog post that it is important to study and "reimagine a canon that is living, breathing, dynamic, and reflective of the world our students live in. Additionally, we move from viewing youth in deficit-centered discourses to understanding youth culture as something worthy of analysis within a classroom space."

When we seek to include the world young people inhabit today in our classroom learning environments, inspiring figures from history are some of the people we look to first. But who are the individuals young people remember from their pasts? Who are the people in their communities they think will be remembered in the future? Who we remember has the power to dictate who we are and who we inspire future generations to become. It is through remembrance that we also recognize events that should never be forgotten and those that have changed the face of history.

Illumination

Here, you have a chance to explore remembrance in your own life. Use the invitations below to engage meaningfully with this month's theme and reflect on what it means to you.

Complete the following phrases.

1. I remember a time when . . . and it has stayed with me because . . .

   _____
   _____
   _____

2. Some of the pieces of literature that I remember most are . . . because . . .

   _____
   _____
   _____

3. What makes a story unforgettable is . . .

   _____
   _____
   _____

Respond to the following questions.

4. Who are some people from your community that you believe will not be forgotten?

   _____
   _____
   _____

5. Why do school curricula mandate the teaching of certain literature for decades or centuries? What might be gained from replacement? What might be lost?

   _____
   _____
   _____

6. What moves do educators need to make to ensure they teach complete histories representing all perspectives?

   _____
   _____
   _____

Investigation

Investigate this month's theme of remembrance with your students by inviting them to complete the following activities. Think and talk about ways you can inspire remembrance with your text choices.

Kindergarten to Fifth Grade

Stories honor our students' experiences and the experiences of others both real and imagined. Consider the impact of stories, both fiction and nonfiction, to unpack history and learn lessons from the rule makers and the rule breakers. Consider the impact of *story* in "history." Lead a discussion with your students based on your reflections and prompt them to consider how stories make up all of history and teach us about ourselves.

Sixth to Eighth Grade

Have students follow these instructions: Investigate an individual or historical event that you consider to be well known or a household name. Then investigate one (or more) who are not as well known or who might be considered "hidden figures." Students might find some of these by using search terms like "little-known musicians" or "visual artists of the [marginalized group of people] diaspora." Students can play with their search terms and see what they discover. Students may also use the books recommended in the Bookshelves pages (pages 116-117) to provide clues that will help them launch research into specific people, events, and places.

Mentor Spotlight: Minh Lê

Minh Lê is the author of *Drawn Together* (2018), a book about family and intergenerational connection across cultural and language divides. Lê also wrote *Enlighten Me* (2023) and *Green Lantern: Legacy* (2020), books that take traditional Eastern storytelling elements and weave them into modern tales that resonate with readers of all ages. Lê's work is deeply influenced by his relationship with his grandparents. His stories often encourage young readers to reflect on their own connections with elders and explore intergenerational relationships. Lê is a strong advocate for children and diverse representation in literature, having served on the board of We Need Diverse Books. His books frequently spark conversations about community and compassion. Lê maintains an active presence on social media, connecting with educators and students. You can read more and learn about him at his website using the following QR code or visit his blog, Minh Lê Books (https://minhlebooks.com/blog), where he provides an annual Extreme Caldecott Placement highlighting some of his favorite picture books of the year. Head over for information on children's literature and invite your students to reflect on their favorite books of the year.

Visit Minh Lê's website using the following QR code.

https://minhlebooks.com

Week One

To Do

Notes

Monday

Tuesday

Wednesday

We do not learn from experience....
We learn from reflecting on experience.

—John Dewey

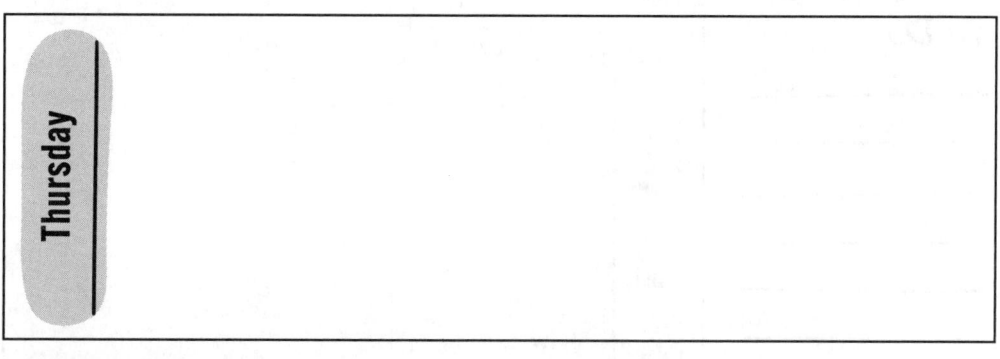

Thursday

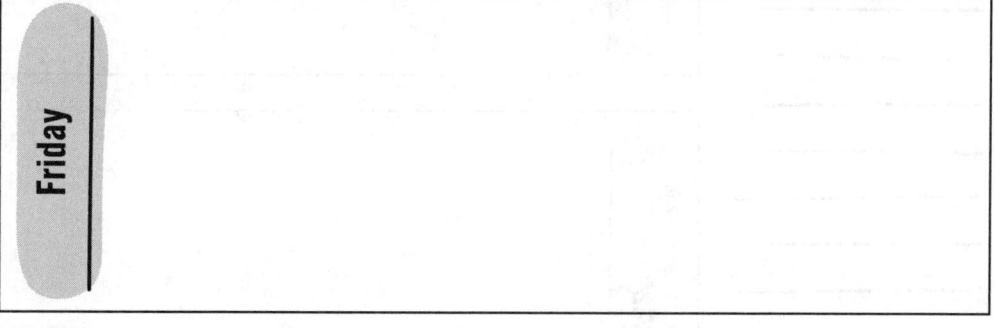

Friday

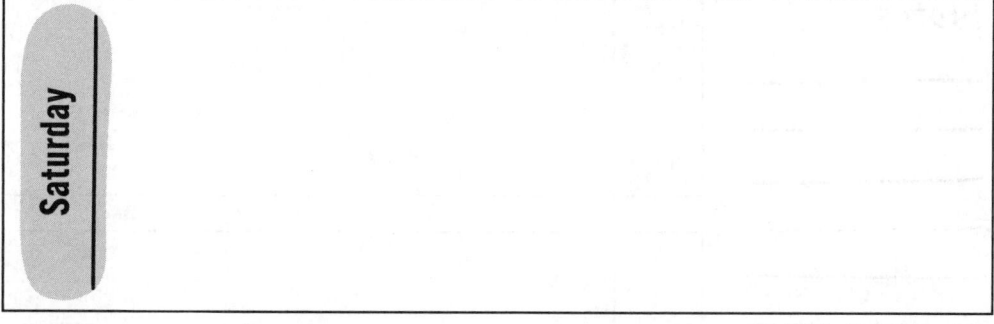

Saturday

Sunday

Week Two

To Do

Notes

Monday

Tuesday

Wednesday

Don't count the days, make the days count.

—Muhammad Ali

Thursday

Friday

Saturday

Sunday

Week Three

To Do

Notes

Monday

Tuesday

Wednesday

I am who I am today because of the choices I made yesterday.

—Eleanor Roosevelt

Thursday

Friday

Saturday

Sunday

Week Four

To Do

Notes

Monday

Tuesday

Wednesday

Memory is the diary we all carry about with us.
—Oscar Wilde

 AUGUST
 SEPTEMBER
 OCTOBER
 NOVEMBER
 DECEMBER
 JANUARY
 FEBRUARY
 MARCH
 APRIL
 MAY
 JUNE
 JULY

Thursday

Friday

Saturday

Sunday

115

December Bookshelves

Title	Author and Illustrator	Teaching Considerations
The Map of Good Memories (2017)	Fran Nuño, illustrated by Zuzanna Celej	Invite students to consider places in their communities and homes that evoke good memories. Students may recall heart maps and writing territories as they craft their writing lives. You may also share this story to spark discussions about refugees, relocation, and the impact of war.
Remembering (2023)	Xelena González, illustrated by Adriana M. Garcia	This story helps with remembering the loss of a loved one. Steeped in the history and tradition of Día de Muertos, it can also serve to help students focus on the loss of a pet or family member.
Together We Remember (2025)	Jackie Morera, illustrated by Violeta Encarnación	This is a story that weaves together family love, loss, grief, and hope. It's a wonderful way to help students recognize the power of stories to celebrate memories and moments (old and new).
Wilfrid Gordon McDonald Partridge (2017, 1984 fortieth anniversary edition)	Mem Fox, illustrated by Julie Vivas	This is an oldie but goodie (originally published 1984) that works well to explore what makes a memory. Invite students to write or discuss all the metaphors for memories provided in this story and how they might connect to "things" they associated with memories they treasure.
Zora, the Story Keeper (2023)	Ebony Joy Wilkins, illustrated by Dare Coulter	This book and its focusing on family and traditions is a great invitation to encourage your students to celebrate through writing, photos, or oral storytelling.

Title	Author and Illustrator	Teaching Considerations
Eagle Drums (2023)	Nasuġraq Rainey Hopson	In this origin story that tells the tale of a Native Alaskan tradition, the Iñupiaq Iḷupiaq Messenger Feast, a young hunter learns about himself and the natural world. Use this text to discuss the importance of origin stories and the role of traditional stories that create shared cultural understandings.
Memory Jars (2021)	Vera Brosgol	This middle grade memoir provides opportunities to discuss savoring our memories and moments.
The Night Diary (2018)	Veera Hiranandani	This book addresses grief and loss as well as the partition of India, when one land was divided into India and Pakistan. Teach about borders and geography and how and why governments divide groups of people who have historically been part of the same communities.
Rising from From the Ashes: Los Angeles, 1992. Edward Jae Song Lee, Latasha Harlins, Rodney King, and a City on Fire (2024)	Paula Yoo	This stirring account of the 1992 Los Angeles uprising examines its impact on Korean and Black communities. Use this text to discuss protest and civil unrest, their causes, and whether they can bring desired solutions.
A Seed in the Sun (2022)	Aida Salazar	This book tells the story of the 1965 protest for migrant workers' rights involving Dolores Huerta. Use it to teach collective action and the role migrant workers have played in building the global economy and food production.
Victory. Stand!: Raising My Fist for Justice (2022)	Tommie Smith and Derrick Barnes, illustrated by Dawud Anyabwile	This graphic novel tells the story of the 1968 Mexico City Olympics and how two men raised their fists for justice and took a stand against anti-Black racism. Use this book to discuss discrimination and colorism, and how these concepts intersect with the stories humans choose to uplift and those that remain hidden.

117

December Bookshelves

Title	Author and Illustrator	Teaching Considerations

Use this blank bookshelf to reflect on books you might like to include in your teaching this month.

Title	Author and Illustrator	Teaching Considerations

Activities and Instructional Moves

Follow the invitations to help share this month's theme with your classroom. You'll find invitations and instructional guidance for elementary (K–5) and intermediate (6–8) students.

Kindergarten to Fifth Grade

- **Reflect on personal growth:** Invite students to look back while also looking forward. Have students consider their achievements since the start of this year. Have them ask themselves, "How have I grown?" Encourage them to reflect a bit on the kind of reader and writer they have been. Then have them ask themselves, "How might I continue to grow? What plans do I have for the upcoming calendar year?"
- **Memory jar:** Invite students to keep track of their favorite memories in a mason jar. They can bring in an object or photograph, create a drawing, or write their favorite memories from school (day, week, month, or year). You may also use it as a reflection and remembrance of the entire year, providing students with time to revisit favorite memories at the end of the school year. See figure 5.1 for an example.

FIGURE 5.1: Memory jar.

Sixth to Eighth Grade

- **Make a "Map of Myself":** Have students create a map of their lives so far, including places that are important to them. They should create a road going through the map so that it illustrates their journey. They might consider including places they've traveled to or imaginary places from dreams or books, places they love and places they go routinely. Instruct them to include captions by each place with detail about what the place means to them and the role it has played in their life.
- **Write a letter to your future self:** Students should write a letter to their future self about anything they want. Make sure they include observations about the present and hopes for the future, as well as some details about what the world is like from their perspective. This may include but is not limited to who is in the government and what they think about them, popular trends, music, TV shows, pastimes, and anything else they think their future self would enjoy reading about. Collect the letters to mail back to students around the time they graduate from high school or collect email addresses if students submit their letters electronically.

End-of-Month Reflection Questions

1. How do we decide who and what should be preserved for the collective memory of communities and societies?
   _____
   _____
   _____

2. Who or what do you think should be remembered but is not currently widely known?
   _____
   _____
   _____

3. What are some of the events that have taken place in your lifetime that you know you will remember forever? Why?
   _____
   _____
   _____

4. What is the role of education in preserving stories?
   _____
   _____
   _____

5. Which stories or texts continue to be remembered and taught? Why?
   _____
   _____
   _____

6. What stories or texts do you think should be replaced in the canon taught in schools? Why?
   _____
   _____
   _____

7. What is the benefit of preserving stories for future generations through the written word? What other ways do we preserve stories?
   _____
   _____
   _____

JANUARY

Calling

Draw the art you want to see, start the business you want to run, play the music you want to hear, write the books you want to read, build the products you want to use—do the work you want to see done.

—**Austin Kleon**

When we are young, the future is full of possibilities. There are any number of potential professions or paths that could shape what some refer to as destiny. In educational environments, we prepare students for a future that is unknown to them. It is wise to remind ourselves that while each individual's calling is unique, there are gifts each person has that make them especially suited to fulfill a purpose. Identifying a calling happens early in life for some and later for others. It is a process that can—and usually does—involve trial and error, successes and failures. Educators can serve as mentors, guides, and coaches, cheering students on and helping them find the courage to keep moving toward their calling, regardless of how implausible or difficult to reach it may seem.

Consider what initially drew you to the field of education and, specifically, teaching literacy. Some might say a calling is a profound sense of direction or purpose that aligns with individual skills and experiences. What experiences have you had with literature that guided you to become a literacy educator? What often draws a person to define teaching as more than a vocation is the intrinsic motivation that comes from working with young people and helping them reach their highest potential. As you read through this month's chapter, seek to discover what makes teaching more than a vocation for you and what you hope to uncover each new year as you rediscover your calling.

The Social Change Ecosystem Map is a tool created by Deepa Iyer (2017) to help people understand their roles in social justice work. It identifies different roles like healer, storyteller, or builder, showing how each person can contribute to positive change in their own way. This map is one of several lenses educators can use to help students identify their unique gifts and how they might use them to work for a just and equitable society. As you read the works curated for you in this month's Bookshelves pages (pages 138–139) and work through the reflection questions, consider how you might support the young people in your life to identify their calling and how they might best prepare to serve humanity.

Important Dates

- National Month of Creativity
- National Book Blitz Month
- National Braille Literacy Month
- ALA Youth Media Award Celebrations (third Monday of January)
- National Science Fiction Day (January 2)
- World Braille Day (January 4)
- National Word Nerd Day (January 9)
- National Thesaurus Day (January 18)
- Library Shelfie Day (fourth Wednesday of January)
- Multicultural Children's Book Day (last Thursday of January)

Looking Ahead: February

- National Black History Month
- National Library Lovers' Month
- The African American Read-In (AARI; month long)
- World Read Aloud Day (first Wednesday of February)

JANUARY

To Do

Notes

	Monday	Tuesday	Wednesday
	○	○	○
	○	○	○
	○	○	○
	○	○	○
	○	○	○

Thursday	Friday	Saturday	Sunday
○	○	○	○
○	○	○	○
○	○	○	○
○	○	○	○
○	○	○	○

Inspiration

Our students are the future. Our societies will be shaped not only by their choices but also by the choices the adults in their lives make regarding them. Therefore, it is important to remember that everyone is part of a continuum and that educators and the students they serve are future ancestors. On the way to discovering one's calling, it is essential to consider larger questions such as the following.

- What mark do you want to leave behind on the world around you?
- How do you want to be remembered?
- What skills do you have that you can best use to serve those around you?

It is also important to remember that the present is not shaped only by people whom the world or online communities choose to prominently showcase. There are many people working behind the scenes to make an impact who are not and do not aspire to be known to everyone.

When thinking about inspiration for a calling, educators should guide young people to notice the everyday small actions that people around them undertake. Guide them to reflect by looking inward, but also by noticing those in their community who inspire and impress them. Don't forget: The process of recognizing a calling begins with combining passion with purpose.

Illumination

Here, you have a chance to explore calling in your own life. Use the invitations below to engage meaningfully with this month's theme and reflect on what it means to you.

1. Who are some of the people in your life whose callings have impacted you?

2. Would you consider yourself to be most easily impactful or impacted? In what ways?

3. When did you first feel moved to work with young people?

4. What callings do you have and how have they shifted over time?

5. How do you influence the people in your life?

6. What gifts do you feel you have that you can use to help others?

Investigation

Investigate this month's theme of calling with your students by inviting them to complete the following activities. Think and talk about ways you can inspire calling with your text choices.

Kindergarten to Fifth Grade

As we continue to engage students in the necessary work of thinking about and beyond texts, we may consider the ways we invite our students to share their thoughts. Devise a calling-based activity for students that considers the following questions.

- How have the people or things you have read about inspired you to grow?

- Do you feel encouraged to share what you think? If so, in what ways? If not, what would help encourage you?
- Do you find value in listening to and learning from your peers? If so, in what ways? If not, what would make such interactions more valuable?
- In what ways can you use texts to consider how you can use your voice, your art, or your words to make an impact on our world?

Sixth to Eighth Grade

Ask students to investigate a profession or job they think they might like to have. Then, invite them to respond to the following prompts in a journal, worksheet, or group discussion.

- What is the history of your chosen role in society?
- Has this role always existed, or has it evolved over time? (For example, nurses and doctors have always existed in some form, whereas a cybersecurity specialist is a relatively new field.)
- What skills, education, or training would you need to serve humanity in this capacity?

Mentor Spotlight: Joanna Ho

Joanna Ho is an author, educator, and speaker whose work reflects her passion for anti-bias, anti-racism, and equity work. As the daughter of immigrants from Taiwan and China, Ho writes stories so "that we understand our own stories, that we can see the ways we are all connected, that we've always been really powerful" (McLernon, 2024). Joanna Ho's books are a celebration of cultural identities, making her a significant influence for aspiring writers. She excels at presenting complex ideas in engaging and accessible ways, particularly through her joyful picture books. Her work reflects a deep commitment to creating positive change in the world.

Visit Joanna Ho's website using the following QR code.

www.joannahowrites.com

129

Week One

To Do

Notes

Monday

Tuesday

Wednesday

> Everyone has a purpose in life...
> a unique gift or special talent to give to others.
>
> —Deepak Chopra

Thursday

Friday

Saturday

Sunday

Week Two

AUGUST

SEPTEMBER

OCTOBER

NOVEMBER

DECEMBER

JANUARY

FEBRUARY

MARCH

APRIL

MAY

JUNE

JULY

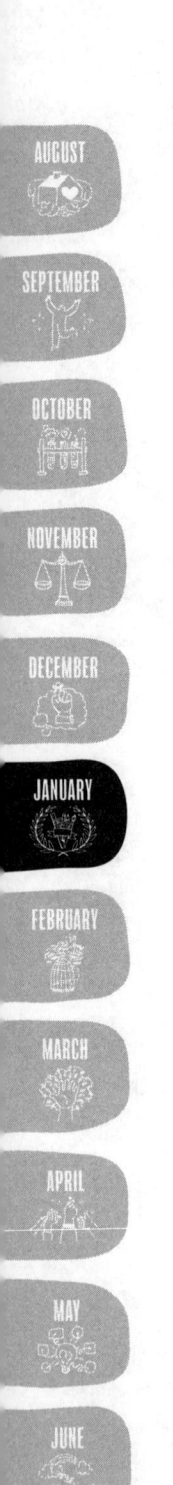

To Do

Notes

Monday

Tuesday

Wednesday

Don't stop learning because there is too much to learn.

—Joanna Ho

Thursday

Friday

Saturday

Sunday

Week Three

To Do

Notes

Monday

Tuesday

Wednesday

Ask yourself what makes you come alive.

—Howard Thurman

Thursday

Friday

Saturday

Sunday

Week Four

To Do

Notes

Monday

Tuesday

Wednesday

Education is for improving the lives of others and for leaving your community and world better than you found it.

—**Marian Wright Edelman**

Thursday

Friday

Saturday

Sunday

AUGUST
SEPTEMBER
OCTOBER
NOVEMBER
DECEMBER
JANUARY
FEBRUARY
MARCH
APRIL
MAY
JUNE
JULY

137

January Bookshelves

Title	Author and Illustrator	Teaching Considerations
Every Month Is a New Year: Celebrations Around the World (2018)	Marilyn Singer, illustrated by Susan L. Roth	Share this poetry collection to reflect on and honor New Year celebrations around the world.
Not Little (2021)	Maya Myers, illustrated by Hyewon Yum	This book will invite conversations about what it means to be an ally or upstander, as well as what it means to have a big heart. Consider sharing its companion, *Not Perfect*, also by Myers and Yum, for more conversations.
The Reflection in Me (2024)	Marc Colagiovanni, illustrated by Peter H. Reynolds	Originally a short film, this story tells about love, self-acceptance, and self-worth. Both the film and the book can provide opportunities to strengthen concepts around all of the above.
Show the World! (2022)	Angela Dalton, illustrated by Daria Peoples	This book is a gorgeous celebration of self-expression centered on Black children. It also serves as an opportunity to reflect with all children on the many ways they can make their own marks in this world.
Something, Someday (2023)	Amanda Gorman, illustrated by Christian Robinson	Poet and activist Amanda Gorman gives us another text to help students reflect on what they might want to see change and how they can create a better future.
The Spark in You (2024)	Andrea Pippins	This title will encourage your students to think about what makes each of us unique and special.

Title	Author and Illustrator	Teaching Considerations
Enlighten Me (2023)	Minh Lê, illustrated by Chan Chau	During a meditation retreat, a young boy finds inner peace and belonging by connecting to stories of the life of Buddha. Use this story to inspire young people to listen to their inner voice.
Front Desk (2019)	Kelly Yang	In this middle grade novel (the first in a series), the ten-year-old protagonist tackles immigrant employee exploitation and economic stability. Use this text to talk about the relationship between power, position in society, and financial empowerment.
Lalani of the Distant Sea (2020)	Erin Entrada Kelly	Twelve-year-old Lalani embarks on an epic journey to save her family and friends. Use this text to talk about breaking gender roles and stereotypes, the power of a hero to inspire, and using gifts to impact the lives of those we care about.
Lety Out Loud (2020)	Angela Cervantes	This text, the second in a series set in an animal shelter, explores what it means to use writing skills to advocate for a cause.
Sal and Gabi Break the Universe (2020)	Carlos Hernandez	Sal can open holes in the space-time continuum. When he meets Gabi, she doesn't believe being a magician is the only use for his abilities. Use this text to explore using our gifts to change the world.

139

January Bookshelves

Title	Author and Illustrator	Teaching Considerations

Use this blank bookshelf to reflect on books you might like to include in your teaching this month.

Title	Author and Illustrator	Teaching Considerations

Activities and Instructional Moves

Follow the invitations to help share this month's theme with your classroom. You'll find invitations and instructional guidance for elementary (K-5) and intermediate (6-8) students.

Kindergarten to Fifth Grade

- **Refocus with reading and writing resolutions:** Consider incorporating into your lesson the suggestion by Donalyn Miller, author of *The Book Whisperer* (2009), to create a list of reading and writing resolutions. Ask students to answer the following questions.
  - What might your list include?
  - How can you refocus to reflect on what you are most passionate about?
  - How might your new goals reflect the ways you can learn from new experiences so that you may grow and give back to your community?

- **Start with one little word:** Building on the idea of resolutions, Ali Edwards (n.d.), blogger and educator, encourages us to capture "one little word" that may help us focus on the things that matter most in our lives. These words may tie to individual or collective goals, such as connect, reflect, listen, pause, family, love, or joy. Brainstorm a list of possibilities with your students and consider creating art projects using that one little word integral to the design. Include student sample ideas to use as a sketch or model.

Sixth to Eighth Grade

- **Explore your passion:** Invite students to explore their passion by responding to the following prompts.
  - What is one thing you've always wanted to do?
  - What has kept you from doing it?

  Ask students to try something new, like a skill (such as roller skating) or a hobby (such as crocheting) that takes time to learn, and keep a diary or video journal of their progress as they develop. Then invite them to reflect on the following question.
  - What kinds of experiences happen on the way to excellence?

  Have students share highlights from their journey with the class.

- **Find your purpose:** Ask students, "Who or what do you most admire? Why?" Then, have them create a visual graphic with a picture of themselves in the middle (this can be a drawing or an actual photograph). Around the outside, have students write words or find pictures that explain who they are, the attributes they feel they have, and those they hope to develop. Then, students will make a circle around these words and images and, on the very outer edge of the graphic, write whom or what they would most like to influence during their life. Create a wall display or gallery walk in your classroom of all the images and get to know your students through their hopes and dreams for the future.

End-of-Month Reflection Questions

1. What moments this month affirmed your understanding of your calling?

   _____

   _____

   _____

2. What are some moments this month that left you questioning or wanting to explore more about your purpose?

   _____

   _____

   _____

3. How will you help young people discover their callings? What goals and action steps might you create for doing so?

   _____

   _____

   _____

4. What stories or experiences have shaped your definition of success? How do you define it?

   _____

   _____

   _____

5. Whom do you think young people in your community look up to? Why?

   _____

   _____

   _____

6. What are the benefits of following a calling? What happens when you don't?

   _____

   _____

   _____

7. How does the world reward those who pursue their dreams?

   _____

   _____

   _____

FEBRUARY

Liberation

Freedom is not something that anybody can be given; freedom is something people take and people are as free as they want to be.

—James Baldwin

Literacy is about more than learning to read and write. Being literate means having the ability to read, write, speak, and gain knowledge and understanding of ourselves and others. We want all our students to see the value in literacy both inside and outside of school. Learning should be lifelong work, emphasizing real-world reading, writing, and critical thinking as keys to self-agency, advocacy, and action. It is this lifelong work that Frederick Douglass (1845/2016) writes about as the foundation of all learning and the pathway to liberation for every human being. When schools align their missions, strategic goals, curricula, and policies to focus on literacy and liberation, they are nurturing the hearts and minds of all students, expanding the view of what literacy is meant to be, and teaching students how to live in this world. This month we invite you to consider the role of liberation in literacy.

Important Dates

- National Black History Month
- National Library Lovers' Month
- The African American Read-In (AARI; month long)
- World Read Aloud Day (first Wednesday of February)
- Take Your Child to the Library Day (first Saturday of February)
- Thank a Mailperson Day (February 4)
- Children's Authors and Illustrators Week (first week of February)
- Read in the Bathtub Day (February 9)
- International Book Giving Day and Library Lovers' Day (February 14)
- Tell a Fairy Tale Day (February 26)
- National Letter to an Elder Day (February 26)

Looking Ahead: March

- National Reading Month
- Small Press Month

FEBRUARY

AUGUST

SEPTEMBER

OCTOBER

NOVEMBER

DECEMBER

JANUARY

FEBRUARY

MARCH

APRIL

MAY

JUNE

JULY

To Do

Notes

Monday	Tuesday	Wednesday
○	○	○
○	○	○
○	○	○
○	○	○
○	○	○

Thursday	Friday	Saturday	Sunday
◯	◯	◯	◯
◯	◯	◯	◯
◯	◯	◯	◯
◯	◯	◯	◯
◯	◯	◯	◯

Inspiration

By exploring complex concepts like liberation, we want students to gain a deeper understanding of what liberation means to all individuals' rights and freedoms. Explore the freedoms our students are privileged to have in this country but ask them to consider those unable to access those liberties. And what about the part of our history that was built on injustice? How can we teach and learn from our past to build a better future?

Illumination

Here, you have a chance to explore liberation in your own life. Use the invitations below to engage meaningfully with this month's theme and reflect on what it means to you.

1. What does it mean to be free? What does freedom mean to you?

2. What freedoms do you cherish and why?

3. Imagine a world without those freedoms. How might things be different for you? For others?

4. Think about a time when you did not feel free. Why was that?

5. Consider the current list of banned books. (If you need help looking for a local or national list, PEN America offers an annual index of books banned in the United States per state, titled the "PEN America Index of School Book Bans," on its website.) From the titles and descriptions of the books that have been banned, what freedoms do you think are being challenged?

6. How does freedom of choice impact your learning?

Investigation

Investigate this month's theme of liberation with your students by inviting them to complete the following activities. Think and talk about ways you can inspire liberation with your text choices.

Kindergarten to Fifth Grade

Have students identify a person or an event in any of the suggested Bookshelves titles (pages 160-161) where their understanding about liberation expanded. Prompt them to answer the following questions.

- In what ways were your ideas about liberation expanded by this book or story?
- How have the stories of real or imagined individuals deepened your understanding and appreciation of what it means to be "free?"

Sixth to Eighth Grade

Have students respond to this prompt as a journal entry, group discussion, or class project: "Explore what you think it means to be liberated through the eyes of young people in your community. Don't forget to consider those who are learning in nontraditional settings (such as juvenile incarceration centers or immigrant detention centers). What do you think it means to liberate another person? How do individuals and societies achieve true liberation?"

Mentor Spotlight: Felicia Rose Chavez

Felicia Rose Chavez's work offers educators a way to depart from traditional writing instruction models and writer's workshops. She models a reflective and decolonial practice that encourages writing instructors to liberate themselves from viewing writing as a set of rules authors must follow to learn to express themselves. Chavez (2021) is the author of *The Antiracist Writing Workshop: How to Decolonize the Creative Classroom*.

Chavez's work focuses on challenging traditional notions of creativity in education. She encourages educators to foster inclusive learning environments and dismantle oppressive systems that hinder student growth and well-being. By understanding how these systems operate in classrooms, educators can take the first step towards creating more equitable and empowering learning communities.

Visit Felicia Rose Chavez's website using the following QR code.

www.antiracistworkshop.com

Week One

To Do

Notes

Monday

Tuesday

Wednesday

The schools we go to are reflections of the society that created them. Nobody is going to give you the education you need to overthrow them.

—Assata Shakur

Thursday

Friday

Saturday

Sunday

AUGUST
SEPTEMBER
OCTOBER
NOVEMBER
DECEMBER
JANUARY
FEBRUARY
MARCH
APRIL
MAY
JUNE
JULY

Week Two

To Do

Notes

Monday

Tuesday

Wednesday

True freedom comes from breaking the chains of oppression.

—**Rigoberta Menchú Tum**

Thursday

Friday

Saturday

Sunday

Week Three

To Do

Notes

Monday

Tuesday

Wednesday

> If you are free, you need to free somebody else.
> If you have some power, then your job is to
> empower somebody else.
>
> —Toni Morrison

Thursday

Friday

Saturday

Sunday

Week Four

To Do

Notes

Monday

Tuesday

Wednesday

Wonder. . . is a force of liberation, it makes sense of what our souls inherently know we were meant for. Every mundane glimpse is salve on a wound, instructions for how to set the bone right again.

—Cole Arthur Riley

Thursday

Friday

Saturday

Sunday

February Bookshelves

Title	Author and Illustrator	Teaching Considerations
Dreams of Freedom in Words and Pictures (2015)	Amnesty International	This thought-provoking collection of art and inspirational quotes illustrates different aspects of human rights.
Every Child a Song: A Celebration of Children's Rights (2020)	Nicola Davies, illustrated by Marc Martin	Using the metaphor of a song, this book provides opportunities to discuss children's rights and other global issues.
Freedom, We Sing (2020)	Amyra León, illustrated by Molly Mendoza	León's poem as a picture book provides repetitive phrases and important questions to help students analyze what freedom means.
Malala's Magic Pencil (2017)	Malala Yousafzai, illustrated by Kerascoët	Learn about the change agent Malala Yousafzai and invite students to explore the impact of literacy, writing, and using one's voice for freedom.
What If One Day . . . (2023)	Bruce Handy and Ashleigh Corrin	This is a fabulous "what-if" conversation starter and a great way to speculate about the future and appreciate what we have.

Title	Author and Illustrator	Teaching Considerations
Art of Protest: Creating, Discovering, and Activating Art for Your Revolution (2021)	De Nichols, illustrated by Diana Dagadita, Molly Mendoza, Olivia Twist, Saddo, and Diego Becas	This book presents and unpacks some of the most important protest art from across the world and throughout history. Analyze visual argument as a means to achieving liberation.
Boxers (2013)	Gene Luen Yang	Teach and learn about the history of the Boxer Rebellion through the eyes of Little Bao and Four-Girl (Vibiana) as they navigate the impact of social revolution and colonization on China. Use this graphic novel to teach about a historical period that is not well known in the West, and what happens when individuals decide to rebel to achieve liberation.
The First Rule of Punk (2018)	Celia C. Pérez	Use this novel to teach about the healing power of creative art to liberate and help individuals break the mold of gender stereotypes or what ideas others hold about who they should be.
Home Is Not a Country (2022)	Safia Elhillo	Use this novel in verse to discuss individual identities within identity groups. This novel is also useful for teaching about the ways individuals can break free from social constructs.
They Call Me Güero: A Border Kid's Poems (2021)	David Bowles	This novel in verse explores the relationship between identity and creativity as well as writing as a tool for self-discovery, self-expression, and liberation.

February Bookshelves

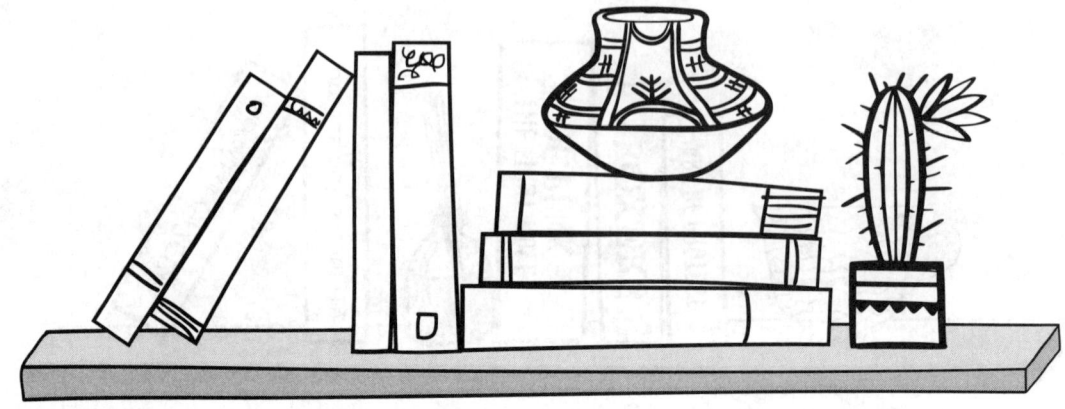

Title	Author and Illustrator	Teaching Considerations

Use this blank bookshelf to reflect on books you might like to include in your teaching this month.

Title	Author and Illustrator	Teaching Considerations

Activities and Instructional Moves

Follow the invitations to help share this month's theme with your classroom. You'll find invitations and instructional guidance for elementary (K-5) and intermediate (6-8) students.

Kindergarten to Fifth Grade

- **Explore liberation:** Consider expanding on the message of freedom and liberation. Invite your students to share their learning through a variety of creative written or artistic responses. For additional inspiration, revisit the art or quotes in Amnesty International's (2015) *Dreams of Freedom in Words and Pictures* or ask students to find their own examples through art, poetry, or stories they find inspiring.

- **List of improvements for the world:** Consider this prompt for students—"Make a list of things you would want to do to improve the world for others." Have students brainstorm with classmates and then write an article, essay, poem, or slogan to capture those ideas.

Sixth to Eighth Grade

- **Create a social media campaign:** Invite your students to create a social media campaign or vlog about a social issue that matters to them involving liberation. This may be as big as a crisis impacting many people or as small and personal as an event impacting individuals at school. Create QR codes that will link to the content and post them at the public library and other places the wider school community will see them.

- **Poll the neighborhood:** Have students make a poll for the community to respond to. While students may collect responses in any format they choose, consider showing them how to use a video library application with curation features to collect video responses. Students can select one of the following topics for the focus of their poll: voter registration, public school lunches and school nutrition, a young person's right to read, or their own topic.

End-of-Month Reflection Questions

1. What makes you feel liberated?
   _____
   _____
   _____

2. How might you use your freedom to advocate for others?
   _____
   _____
   _____

3. What freedoms have you taken for granted?
   _____
   _____
   _____

4. What would you like to see change in our world?
   _____
   _____
   _____

5. How can you make changes happen for yourself and others?
   _____
   _____
   _____

End-of-Month Reflection Questions

MARCH

Renewal

Change is definitely going to happen, no matter what we plan or expect or hope for or set in place. We will adapt to that change, or we will become irrelevant.

—Adrienne Maree Brown

March always comes in like a lion and goes out like a lamb, right? So, if you find yourself wanting to roar this month, consider the ways we can help students and educators feel refreshed and motivated all year long. When we focus on making the days count, and not counting down the days, every moment matters. Attitude is everything. This month we invite you to take the time to help your students and yourself refocus to keep positive energy, joy, and love in all that you do inside and outside of your school space.

Important Dates

- National Reading Month
- Small Press Month
- Greek American Heritage Month
- Irish American Heritage Month
- Read an Ebook Week (first full week of March)
- Read Across America Day (March 2)
- National Write Your Story Day (March 14)
- Freedom of Information Day (March 16)
- World Storytelling Day (March 20)
- World Poetry Day (March 21)

Looking Ahead: April

- National Poetry Month
- National DEAR (Drop Everything and Read) Month
- School Library Month

MARCH

To Do

_____
_____
_____
_____
_____
_____
_____
_____

Notes

_____
_____
_____
_____
_____
_____
_____
_____
_____
_____

Monday	Tuesday	Wednesday
○	○	○
○	○	○
○	○	○
○	○	○
○	○	○

Thursday	Friday	Saturday	Sunday
○	○	○	○
○	○	○	○
○	○	○	○
○	○	○	○
○	○	○	○

Inspiration

Educators have the privilege of experiencing a fresh start annually, at the beginning of each school year. This can be among the most memorable times of the year. Getting to know students and imagining the possibilities that lie ahead both bring a sense of joy. It's invigorating to start a new project, but that sense of joy can dwindle by midyear if we don't stay intentionally energized. We need to keep the promise of a teacher's optimism, enthusiasm, time, and energy all year long. This month, we encourage you to think back to those first-day feelings to renew that promise. Reframe problems as opportunities. What can you change to refocus and renew your commitment to making learning fun for you and for your students?

Illumination

Here, you have a chance to explore renewal in your own life. Use the invitations below to engage meaningfully with this month's theme and reflect on what it means to you.

1. Recall the times that you felt most excited about your work with students. Why was that? What steps might you take to maintain or get that feeling back?

2. Reflect on the writing and art that have most influenced your work. Revisit them to explore further. How might those things influence your work now? What has changed? What might need to change and why?

3. Reflect on some of your goals this year. Have you made progress toward achieving them? What might you continue to do or what might you change?

4. How do you foster a growth mindset in yourself and in your students?

5. What aspects of your physical, emotional, and social habits might benefit from a refresh?

Investigation

Investigate this month's theme of renewal with your students by inviting them to complete the following activities. Think and talk about ways you can inspire renewal with your text choices.

Kindergarten to Fifth Grade

Have students make a list of people who have challenged or inspired them to be a better version of themselves. Prompt them to answer the following questions on a piece of paper.

- In what ways have these people changed you?
- What have you learned or unlearned from those people?
- Have you been influenced by something that someone said or did? How did that experience, event, or text challenge you to grow?

Sixth to Eighth Grade

Have students respond to this prompt: "Journal about at least three distinct events in your life that have changed your perspective. What happened? Who was involved? How did you change or adapt to the circumstances? Consider ways that you became a new version of yourself each time something happened that you cannot forget. Create a visual representation of this change accompanied by quotes from your journal entries. As a bonus, host an art show for the community with the pieces created by the class."

Mentor Spotlight: Anton Treuer

Anton Treuer is an Ojibwe scholar, author, and educator. He educates the world about the importance of cultural preservation through language. His YouTube channel (www.youtube.com/@anton.treuer) teaches the art of cultural preservation through topics like racial equity and Ojibwe culture, history, and language. Anton Treuer's work challenges common misconceptions about Native American culture and language. Through his YouTube channel and books, he presents a vibrant and contemporary view of Native people, particularly the Ojibwe, emphasizing their ongoing traditions and contributions. This approach encourages a deeper understanding and appreciation of Indigenous American life today, moving away from stereotypical portrayals that focus on the past.

Treuer's work serves as a valuable resource for educators to teach young people about the importance of cultural affirmation and respect for diverse communities. As Treuer said in an interview about his work, "Language can disrupt the glue for colonial thinking which has been fundamentally dehumanizing to Indigenous people" (Pember, 2019).

Visit Anton Treuer's website using the following QR code.

www.antontreuer.com

Week One

To Do

Notes

Monday

Tuesday

Wednesday

I don't see the desert as barren at all; I see it as full and ripe. It doesn't need to be flattered with rain. It certainly needs rain, but it does with what it has and creates amazing beauty.

—Joy Harjo

Thursday

Friday

Saturday

Sunday

Week Two

To Do

Notes

Monday

Tuesday

Wednesday

Revolution is not a one-time event.

—Audre Lorde

 AUGUST

 SEPTEMBER

 OCTOBER

 NOVEMBER

 DECEMBER

 JANUARY

 FEBRUARY

 MARCH

 APRIL

 MAY

 JUNE

 JULY

Thursday

Friday

Saturday

Sunday

Week Three

To Do

Notes

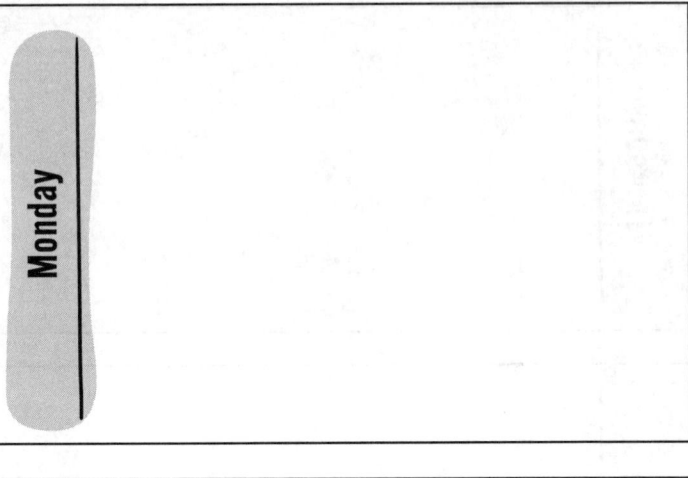
Monday

Tuesday

Wednesday

Every moment is an organizing opportunity, every person a potential activist, every minute a chance to change the world.

—**Dolores Huerta**

Thursday

Friday

Saturday

Sunday

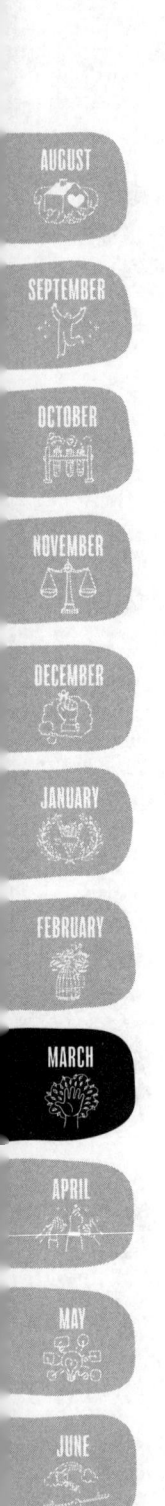
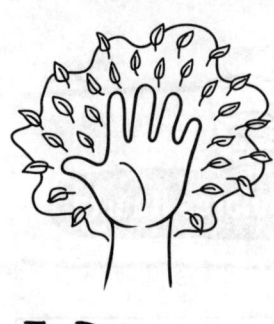

Week Four

To Do

Notes

Monday

Tuesday

Wednesday

We don't even know how strong we are until we are forced to bring that hidden strength forward. In times of tragedy, war, of necessity, people do amazing things. The human capacity for survival and renewal is awesome.

—Isabel Allende

Thursday

Friday

Saturday

Sunday

March Bookshelves

Title	Author and Illustrator	Teaching Considerations
The OK Book (2007)	Amy Krouse Rosenthal, illustrated by Tom Lichtenheld	With its clever visual personification of the word "OK," this book invites conversations about our individual strengths and encourages learners to try new things.
Please, Louise (2014)	Toni Morrison and Slade Morrison, illustrated by Shadra Strickland	Share this story to explore the transformative power of books. Invite your students to reflect on books as friends for exploring, thinking, dreaming, or learning more, and which speaks most to them.
Rain Before Rainbows (2020)	Smriti Prasadam-Halls, illustrated by David Litchfield	Read this story to encourage your students to look for the brighter side of things. Explore challenges, changes, and the power of positive thinking.
Saturday (2019)	Oge Mora	This mother-and-daughter story provides space for children to reflect on those "splendid" precious moments we have spending time with those we love. As a bonus, this book helps students with coping skills and mindfulness in face of disappointments.
This Book Is My Best Friend (2023)	Robin Robinson	Two readers share their reasons for loving the same book. Use this book to teach about perspective, opinion, and being open to the connections and friendships we can find from books and people!

Title	Author and Illustrator	Teaching Considerations
Before the Ever After (2022)	Jacqueline Woodson	In this story about a young boy whose father has suffered a traumatic brain injury, young readers will learn about the enduring power of love to help overcome changes we do not choose, but that choose us.
Darius the Great Is Not Okay (2019)	Adib Khorram	This coming-of-age story will help educators teach about leaving what is familiar to find a new version of yourself and the importance of self-acceptance and supportive friends and family.
Falling Short (2023)	Ernesto Cisneros	Use this story about two best friends living through life challenges and insecurities while navigating the beginning of sixth grade to teach how adversity can bring out the best in us and how recognizing our unique qualities can bring renewed self-worth.
Girls Who Green the World: Thirty-Four Rebel Women Out to Save Our Planet (2022)	Diana Kapp, illustrated by Ana Jarén	This nonfiction compilation contains profiles of thirty-four women who are environmental changemakers, social entrepreneurs, visionaries, and activists. Use this book to inspire, activate, and radicalize future changemakers with fresh perspectives.
Treaty Words: For as Long as the Rivers Flow (2021)	Aimée Craft, illustrated by Luke Swinson	Use this nonfiction book to help students understand that treaties are foundational for creating a culture of reciprocity, respect, responsibility, and renewal.

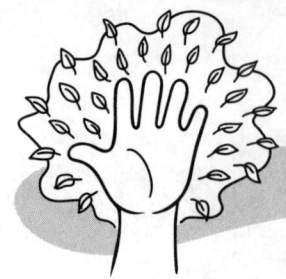

March Bookshelves

Title	Author and Illustrator	Teaching Considerations

Use this blank bookshelf to reflect on books you might like to include in your teaching this month.

Title	Author and Illustrator	Teaching Considerations

Activities and Instructional Moves

Follow the invitations to help share this month's theme with your classroom. You'll find invitations and instructional guidance for elementary (K–5) and intermediate (6–8) students.

Kindergarten to Fifth Grade

- **Think about language:** In his books *Opening Minds* and *Choice Words*, Peter Johnston (2012, 2024) invites us to consider the impact of social-emotional learning, mindset, and language on students viewing themselves in new ways. Think about the language that helps students consider their mistakes as valuable lessons to be learned. Make a chart or graphic with your students that has two sides, one reading "I used to (think, do) . . ." and the other "But now I . . ." Encourage them to find examples from their own experiences and write about or draw what they have learned from this shift in mindset. See figure 8.1 for an example.

- **Watch a TedTalk:** Consider sharing the TedTalk by thirteen-year-old May May Sang (2021) as she reflects on the power of positive thinking. Invite your students to write, verbalize, or record their own ideas on improving their mindsets and share the things they would like to improve (and perhaps steps they will take) to make the most of their own learning journeys.

FIGURE 8.1: Mistakes as learned lessons.

Sixth to Eighth Grade

- **Study your school:** Have students research ways your school has changed since it was first opened—perhaps changes have happened in the physical space as much as the people in the space have changed. What is your school called and why? What is its mission? Who is represented among the staff? Have students investigate how your school environment or another selected knowledge institution (museum, college, library, and so on) has evolved to reflect the people it serves. Then, have students create a map of change detailing different moments in time or important people who have made changes to the institution and been a key part of its evolution.

- **Generate a poetry cycle:** Have students write a poetry cycle documenting three different time periods. The *Encyclopedia Britannica* defines a poetry cycle as a collection of related stories, poems, or narratives, often by various writers, that focus on a legendary hero and the people around them. The term "cyclic poems" originally described poems that continued the story of the Trojan War after Homer (The Editors of Encyclopedia Britannica, 1998). Students can write about events in their lives or on more general topics such as the seasons. Have students focus on sensory details. Students may consider using an organizational acronym like TPFAST (title, paraphrase, figurative language, attitude, shift, and title again) either to help generate thoughts or analyze a partner's poems as part of a peer review process. See figure 8.2 for an example.

TPFAST	Explanation in my own words	Quotes from the poem to support what I think
T *(Title—What is your first interpretation of the title?)*		
P *(Paraphrase—After reading the poem, what do you think it means?)*		
F *(Figurative language—What examples of symbols, imagery, sensory detail, similes, or metaphors can you find?)*		
A *(Attitude—What is the speaker's attitude toward the subject?)*		
S *(Shift—Is there a point where the subject or syntax of the poem changes?)*		
T *(Title again—What is your interpretation of the title now that you've read the poem all the way through?)*		

FIGURE 8.2: TPFAST graphic organizer.

*Visit **go.SolutionTree.com/literacy** for a free reproducible version of this figure.*

End-of-Month Reflection Questions

1. How do you feel about change?

2. What is something that helps you refocus? Why do you think it affects you that way?

3. What actions can you take to rest, reset, and take time out? What happens when you take such actions?

4. What new habits might you add to your routines? Why?

5. Who or what helps you stay motivated? Who or what feeds your energy, enthusiasm, and optimism for this work? Why?

APRIL

Affirmation

As we go back to school, how will you affirm your students?

—Dena Simmons

TEAM LIFT

This month we encourage you to continue to leverage literacy to help your students identify their own inner strengths and recognize and value the strengths of others. *Oxford English Dictionary* defines *affirmation* (n.d.) as "emotional support or encouragement." The act of affirming our students supports them in building confidence within themselves. It also helps them build trust for their instructor as a guide who will help them navigate the times of struggle and triumph that are inevitable parts of education.

When we intentionally thread literacy connections with social-emotional learning and well-being, we can better serve students by promoting positive thinking, building confidence, and increasing self-esteem to help them feel valued. And as we honor individual talents and self-worth, we should also provide a space to reflect on areas for growth and acknowledge the ways we can lift each other up as we explore more complex issues together.

Important Dates

- School Library Month
- National Poetry Month
- National DEAR (Drop Everything and Read) Month
- Neurodiversity Celebration Month
- Autism Appreciation Month
- Arab American Heritage Month
- National Library Week
- National Library Workers Day (Tuesday of National Library Week)
- National Library Outreach Day (Wednesday of National Library Week)
- International Children's Book Day (April 2)
- National School Librarian Day (April 4)
- International Haiku Poetry Day (April 17)
- Earth Day (April 22)
- World Book and Copyright Day (April 23)
- Independent Bookstore Day (last Saturday of April)
- Children's Day (Mundial del Niño; April 30)
- Global Youth Service Day (April 30)

Looking Ahead: May

- Short Story Month
- Children's Book Week

APRIL

To Do

Notes

Monday	Tuesday	Wednesday
○	○	○
○	○	○
○	○	○
○	○	○
○	○	○

Thursday	Friday	Saturday	Sunday
○	○	○	○
○	○	○	○
○	○	○	○
○	○	○	○
○	○	○	○

Inspiration

When we foster inclusive communities that respect and celebrate individual differences, we facilitate learning that honors multiple perspectives and strengthens our love of self and others. In her well-known TED Talk *The Danger of a Single Story*, award-winning author Chimamanda Ngozi Adichie (2009) reminds us of the following:

> There's something wonderful and affirming about reading about your own reality and reading what is familiar to you. And that particular pleasure should never be denied anyone. But it is equally affirming to read about people who are *not* like you.

In what ways might you "read" your students? Think about your instruction. Gather inspiration from the suggested texts and activities. What might you adjust to better work toward affirming your diverse classroom communities, families, and varying aspects of individual identities?

Illumination

Here, you have a chance to explore affirmation in your own life. Use the invitations below to engage meaningfully with this month's theme and reflect on what it means to you.

1. Share the qualities you love most about yourself and why.

   _____
   _____
   _____

Complete the following phrases.

2. I am confident because . . .

   _____
   _____
   _____

3. I feel safe and most capable when . . .

   _____
   _____
   _____

4. I can work through issues by . . .

   _____
   _____
   _____

5. I feel most motivated when . . .

   _____
   _____
   _____

Investigation

Investigate this month's theme of affirmation with your students by inviting them to complete the following activities. Think and talk about ways you can inspire affirmation with your text choices.

Kindergarten to Fifth Grade

Have students select a character or several characters from the titles on the Bookshelves pages (pages 204-205). Then, ask them to reflect on the ways various aspects of their identities were affirmed or challenged. Have students make a list and think about what contributed to those feelings and how they might feel the same or different and why. What other circumstances contribute to those feelings?

Sixth to Eighth Grade

Have students conduct an interview with someone they admire or create a survey for their community. Begin by asking students to come up with at least five interview questions they can ask an interview subject about different places, people, or words that make them feel affirmed. Here are some examples of such questions.

- What is a place other than school where you go to learn about new ideas?
- How do you share your knowledge? What patterns do you notice?
- What similarities are there between ages and other groups of people? What differences do you observe?

As a bonus, have students create a multimedia presentation to share their data with others in your community.

Mentor Spotlight: Katie Yamasaki

Katie Yamasaki is a muralist, author, and teacher who uses art to explore themes of identity and social justice. Her work often focuses on marginalized communities, particularly those affected by mass incarceration. Through her murals, she creates spaces for dialogue and amplifies the voices of those impacted by social injustice. Yamasaki's art serves as a powerful reminder of the importance of representation and the role of art in fostering empathy and understanding. As her biography states, "Yamasaki's greatest hope is that her work will shine a light on communities and individuals who have been pushed to the margins of society, so that we might all be able to see one another more clearly and completely" (Yamasaki, 2021a).

Visit Katie Yamasaki's website using the following QR code.

www.katieyamasaki.com/theartist

# Week One

To Do

Notes

Monday

Tuesday

Wednesday

When one person says, "Yeah, me, too," it gives permission for others to open up.

—Tarana Burke

Thursday

Friday

Saturday

Sunday

Week Two

To Do

_____
_____
_____
_____
_____
_____
_____
_____
_____
_____

Notes

_____
_____
_____
_____
_____
_____
_____
_____
_____
_____
_____
_____

Monday

Tuesday

Wednesday

Having a superpower has nothing to do with the ability to fly or jump, or superhuman strength. The truest superpowers are the ones we all possess: willpower, integrity, and most importantly, courage.

—Jason Reynolds

Thursday

Friday

Saturday

Sunday

Week Three

To Do

Notes

Monday

Tuesday

Wednesday

You are imperfect, you are wired for struggle, but you are worthy of love and belonging.

—Brené Brown

Thursday
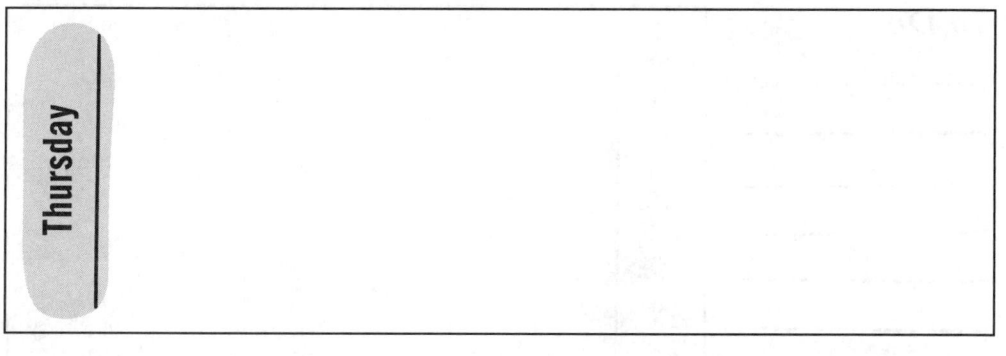

Friday
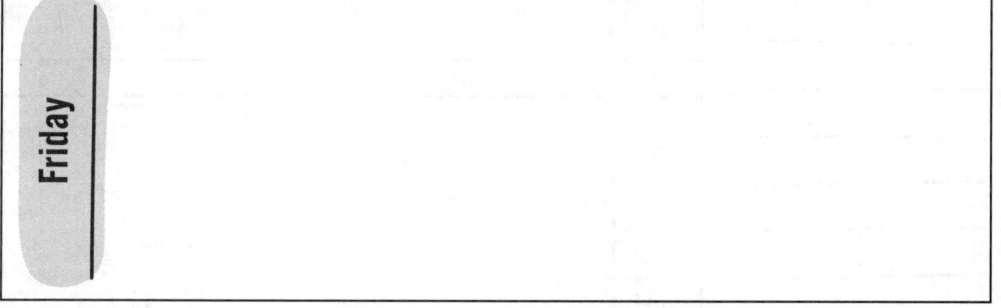

Saturday
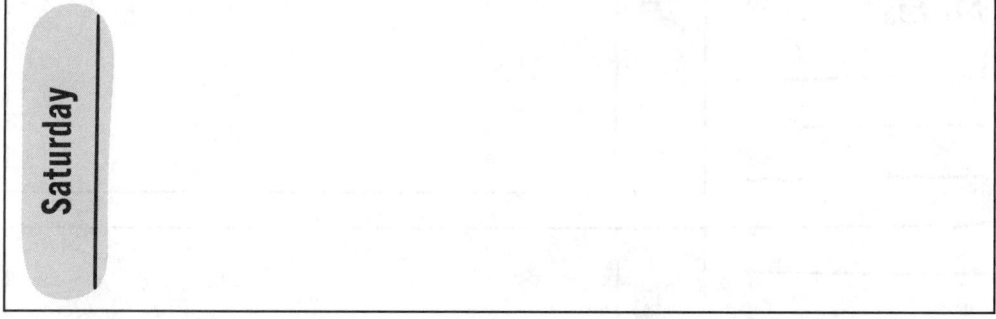

Sunday

Week Four

To Do

Notes

Monday

Tuesday

Wednesday

Hope is a discipline.

—**Mariame Kaba**

Thursday

Friday

Saturday

Sunday

April Bookshelves

Title	Author and Illustrator	Teaching Considerations
The Boy & the Bindi (2016)	Vivek Shraya, illustrated by Rajni Perera	In addition to being a celebration of South Asian culture, this book offers readers an opportunity to celebrate varying gender roles, inclusivity, and individuality.
Dad Bakes (2021)	Katie Yamasaki	This delightful picture book about a dad's relationship with his daughter can help teach about the importance of stories that break through gender stereotypes and affirm all types of families, including those in which a caregiver has been affiliated with the criminal justice system.
Five Words That Are Mine (2024)	Melissa Seron Richardson, illustrated by Addy Rivera Sonda	Mia searches for "cinco palabras" (five words) to describe herself and serves as an inspiration for students to consider which powerful words and in what languages they would use to do the same.
I Am! Affirmations for Resilience (2020)	Bela Barbosa, illustrated by Edel Rodriguez	This board book is the perfect tool to begin conversations about affirmations, with statements and movements to lift students up on their journeys in life.
I Am! A Book of Reminders (2022)	Juana Medina	The text and pictures in this book, part of the "I Will!" series, will help our youngest learners build emotional literacy skills, confidence, and self-esteem.
I'm From (2023)	Gary R. Gray Jr., illustrated by Oge Mora	This book takes a poetic look at the people, places, and things that define who we are and where we are from. It's a great text to invite conversations about belonging and taking pride in one's identities.
Who I Am: Words I Tell Myself (2023)	Susan Verde, illustrated by Peter H. Reynolds	This is a collection of positive affirmations and a celebration of self-love. Share this book to help students own the things that make them special.

Title	Author and Illustrator	Teaching Considerations
Ana on the Edge (2021)	A. J. Sass	This middle grade novel about a figure skater exploring nonbinary identity can teach all readers about the importance of cultivating friendships with people who will affirm who we are and see us in our best light.
King and the Dragonflies (2022)	Kacen Callender	In the Louisiana bayou, a young boy tackles grief, familial unrest, and social rejection on the way to self-discovery and learning there's no right way to be himself.
Nuestra América: 30 Inspiring Latinas/Latinos Who Have Shaped the United States (2020)	Sabrina Vourvoulias, illustrated by Gloria Félix	In collaboration with the Smithsonian Latino Center, this collection (also available in Spanish) affirms Latine identity by highlighting contributions of over thirty notable individuals. Use this text to kick off investigating other anthologies that illuminate notable individuals, their lives, and their achievements.
Swim Team (2022)	Johnnie Christmas	A middle school girl faces her fears and learns perseverance as she becomes her school's best chance at beating its rival. Use this story to teach about Black identity, the history of racial segregation in swimming, and how sports can be a path to social and personal affirmation.
This Place: 150 Years Retold (2019)	Kateri Akiwenzie-Damm, Sonny Assu, Brandon Mitchell, Rachel Qitsualik-Tinsley, Sean Qitsualik-Tinsley, and colleagues.	This graphic novel anthology of Canada's history affirms Indigenous readers and informs all people about the many ways First Nations people have survived since first contact. Read about creativity, imagination, perseverance, and present-day survival as ways to preserve and affirm identity.

April Bookshelves

Title	Author and Illustrator	Teaching Considerations

Use this blank bookshelf to reflect on books you might like to include in your teaching this month.

Title	Author and Illustrator	Teaching Considerations

Activities and Instructional Moves

Follow the invitations to help share this month's theme with your classroom. You'll find invitations and instructional guidance for elementary (K-5) and intermediate (6-8) students.

Kindergarten to Fifth Grade

- **Display an affirmation station:** Consider creating an affirmation station (either by yourself or have students help you) to display pictures and words that illustrate things that make people special and showcase inner and outer strengths. Figure 9.1 shows an example created by preschoolers and kindergartners inspired by "I am" statements from some of our Bookshelves titles (pages 204-205).

- **Create crafts:** Invite your students to revisit and explore the craft lessons and mentor sentences found in Gary R. Gray Jr.'s (2023) *I'm From* picture book. You may want to share as examples the videos "Where You From?" by Renée Watson (2022) and "I Am a Poet" by Charles R. Smith Jr. (2013), both on YouTube, to encourage your students to write or perform with their own models of affirming poetry about their own lives.

FIGURE 9.1: Affirmation station.

Sixth to Eighth Grade

- **Display an affirmation wall:** Make a wall of affirmation (or have your students create one) for people in students' families, their classroom, or the school community. You might use sticky notes and arrange them in the shape of a heart. Alternatively, consider making it look like the affirmation wall at the Seattle Public Library, which encourages visitors to leave a note or affirmation or take one as needed. See figure 9.2 for a visual model.

- **Write a blackout poem:** A *blackout poem* is a new poem constructed by blacking out words in an existing poem (Robles, n.d.). Have students use part of their favorite poem to create their own blackout poem that affirms someone. Students can also write their own affirming poem and illustrate it. You might consider showing students Mahogany L. Browne's (2016) *Black Girl Magic* as an example.

FIGURE 9.2: Affirmation wall.

End-of-Month Reflection Questions

1. How will you continue to connect students' ownership of their learning to themes of affirmation?

   _____
   _____
   _____

2. In what ways have you grown in your understanding of yourself and your students?

   _____
   _____
   _____

3. What texts or activities will you revisit to strengthen your emotional well-being and that of your students?

   _____
   _____
   _____

4. What music, art, and other resources may influence your choices in lesson planning?

   _____
   _____
   _____

5. Think about the places, people, and experiences that help you feel most valued. Why do they help you feel that way?

   _____
   _____
   _____

MAY

....

Possibility

The limits of the possible can only be defined by going beyond them into the impossible.

—Arthur C. Clarke

Looking back over this year, you will find common threads that promote reflection, foster growth, and empower students in taking ownership of their learning journeys. We want students to have a tremendous sense of agency. It calls to mind choose-your-own-adventure books. What path will your students take? When we remain curious, are willing to take chances, learn from our mistakes, and focus on learning as lifework, the possibilities are endless.

Educators need to create lasting literacy that goes beyond the classroom walls. Our students need to understand reading and writing as essential skills in life. Our teaching and learning communities grow when they empower students who are intellectually, socially, emotionally, and politically dedicated to improving themselves and our society through their experiences as readers, writers, and thinkers.

Important Dates

- Asian American, Native Hawaiian, and Pacific Islander Heritage Month
- Get Caught Reading Month (visit https://getcaughtreading.org)
- Mental Health Awareness Month
- Short Story Month
- Jewish American Heritage Month
- Teacher Appreciation Week (first full week of May)
- World Laughter Day (first Sunday of May)
- Memorial Day (last Monday of May)
- Children's Book Week (first week of May)
- World Press Freedom Day (May 3)
- National Cartoonist Day (May 5)
- Free Comic Book Day (first Saturday of May)
- National Limerick Day (May 12)

Looking Ahead: June

- Rainbow Book Month
- National Audiobook Appreciation Month
- Immigrant Heritage Month

MAY

To Do

Notes

Monday	Tuesday	Wednesday
○	○	○
○	○	○
○	○	○
○	○	○
○	○	○

Thursday	Friday	Saturday	Sunday
○	○	○	○
○	○	○	○
○	○	○	○
○	○	○	○
○	○	○	○

Inspiration

With every text our students read and write, they are invited to make choices. What would you do? What do you think? As readers and writers, we consider topics, content, and genre in our reading selections and craft choices in our writing. We know those choices may be vastly different based on interests, readiness levels, needs, learning styles, and preferences. Only one thing remains the same: Choice empowers. This month, we invite you to reflect on the boundless potential of choices to learn in community and expand students' access to information, diverse perspectives, and exploration of new ideas. Those experiences afford us small, everyday choices to write our own adventures.

Illumination

Here, you have a chance to explore possibility in your own life. Use the invitations below to engage meaningfully with this month's theme and reflect on what it means to you.

1. Reflect on individuals (in your life, in history) that have seemingly achieved the impossible. What lessons can you take from their experiences?

   _____
   _____
   _____

2. As you explore new opportunities, what drives you—courage, perseverance, passion, or something else? What would you add and why?

   _____
   _____
   _____

3. We are never done learning. Who or what has had the greatest influence on you in trying something new? How has that influence affected your willingness to try new things?

   _____
   _____
   _____

4. Think about areas outside of your expertise. What have you tried that felt impossible? What did you learn most about yourself in your trials?

   _____
   _____
   _____

5. Complete this sentence: When you believe anything is possible . . .

   _____
   _____
   _____

Investigation

Investigate this month's theme of possibility with your students by inviting them to complete the following activities. Think and talk about ways you can inspire possibility with your text choices.

Kindergarten to Fifth Grade

Often authors and illustrators share their "impossible" journeys to getting published. They may write about their creative process in the book's back matter or offer little-known and inspirational stories in their author's notes. Share an author's note with students that will help inspire them or invite your students to research behind the book and share fun facts from their favorite creators with the class. For those who would like to extend the activity, suggest students review a recent piece of their own writing and add similar information as they found in the author's notes they collected. Perhaps they have an additional message for their readers, a timeline, or a source to explore for further information. Allow students time to share and expand on these ideas alone or in small groups.

Sixth to Eighth Grade

Many science fiction authors begin by imagining possibilities. Ask students, "What scientific principle or principle of nature would you change if you could?" Then have them look for a short story or identify in one of the titles from the Bookshelves pages (pages 226-227) this month that bends the rules of reality or stretches possibilities. Students can use their selection as inspiration for their own story, or journal about what the world would be like if things we accept as impossible were actually possible. For example, what if rain fell up instead of down?

Mentor Spotlight: Antero Garcia

Antero Garcia is a language arts teacher and associate professor at Stanford University who conducts research focused on the intersection between "play, civics, justice, and imagination" (Garcia, n.d.), creating a bridge between current-day practices and how education might evolve if we make space for creativity, play, and imagination. He co-designed the Critical Design and Gaming School in Los Angeles, a public high school that integrates play, imagination, and social justice into its curriculum. Garcia's work highlights the power of intrinsic motivation and creative learning experiences. He is a sought-after speaker at conferences and workshops, inspiring educators to reimagine their teaching practices. Garcia has authored numerous books and served as a classroom ambassador for the U.S. Department of Education.

Visit Antero Garcia's website using the following QR code.

www.anterogarcia.com

Week One

To Do

Notes

Monday

Tuesday

Wednesday

> All things are possible until they are proved impossible.
> Even the impossible may only be so, as of now.
>
> —Pearl S. Buck

Thursday

Friday

Saturday

Sunday

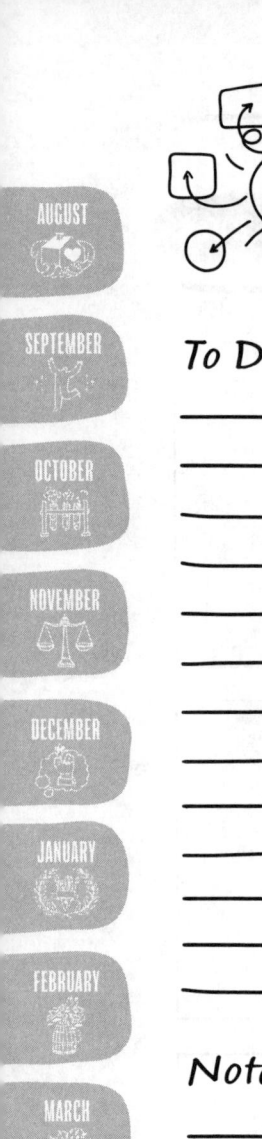

Week Two

To Do

Notes

Monday

Tuesday

Wednesday

In order to rise from its own ashes, a Phoenix first must burn.

—Octavia E. Butler

Thursday

Friday

Saturday

Sunday

221

Week Three

To Do

Notes

Monday

Tuesday

Wednesday

In the beginner's mind there are many possibilities, but in the expert's mind there are few.

—Shunryū Suzuki

Thursday

Friday

Saturday

Sunday

Week Four

To Do

Notes

Monday

Tuesday

Wednesday

Each of us has the right, the possibility, to invent ourselves daily. If a person does not invent herself she will be invented. So, to be bodacious enough to invent ourselves is wise.

—Maya Angelou

Thursday

Friday

Saturday

Sunday

May Bookshelves

Title	Author and Illustrator	Teaching Considerations
The Curious Why (2024)	Angela DiTerlizzi, illustrated by Lorena Alvarez Gómez	Share this playful, rhyming text (a companion to *The Magical Yet*, 2020, also by DiTerlizzi and Gómez) to help students be more open to exploring the world around them. This work inspires reflection and sparks students' interests, helping them engage in more activities.
The End Is Just the Beginning (2022)	Mike Bender, illustrated by Diana Mayo	As a twist, this tale starts with the end. It's a great opportunity to get students thinking in new ways about a variety of topics. Use this text to invite conversations around changes and challenges through the lens of hope and optimism.
Maybe: A Story About the Endless Potential in All of Us (2019)	Kobi Yamada, illustrated by Gabriella Barouch	This inspiring and affirming story is a celebration of possibilities.
Two Truths and a Lie: It's Alive! (2017)	Ammi-Joan Paquette and Laurie Ann Thompson	This innovative informational text explores the playful concept of sharing two truths and a lie. This book can serve as a unique mentor text for writing or speaking about a variety of subjects.
What the Road Said (2021)	Cleo Wade, illustrated by Lucie de Moyencourt	Share this story and its encouraging message to consider all the possible paths on life's journey.

Title	Author and Illustrator	Teaching Considerations
The First State of Being (2024)	Erin Entrada Kelly	Ridge is the world's first time traveler. Michael is a boy with anxiety, doomsday prepping like there's no tomorrow. Travel with Michael and Ridge as they navigate the infinite possibilities of an unknown past and uncertain future. This book shows how found family can help us make the right choices and find our true path.
The Last Mirror on the Left (2020)	Lamar Giles, illustrated by Dapo Adeola	Travel with the Alton boys to a parallel dimension where all is different from the world they know. Use this book, the first in a fun, action-packed series, to teach about the criminal justice system and how to stretch the limits of possibility when we consider what might be rather than only what is.
Star Child: A Biographical Constellation of Octavia Estelle Butler (2022)	Ibi Zoboi	This biography of Octavia Butler, told as a novel in verse, gives readers an intimate view of the visionary author's life and works. Use it to teach about expanding the world of possibilities we live in through the creative arts.
Trickster: Native American Tales—A Graphic Collection (2021, tenth anniversary edition)	Matt Dembicki (editor)	These Native American tales feature tricksters (beings that can both create and destroy) told from the perspectives of various tribal traditions. Teach about the common elements of a trickster and the way people use stories to create shared meaning across cultural traditions.
You Only Live Once, David Bravo (2022)	Mark Oshiro	Eleven-year-old David Bravo wants a do-over of a no good, very bad day. Read this book and discuss how day-to-day choices impact the fabric of our lives with both short- and long-term consequences.

May Bookshelves

Title	Author and Illustrator	Teaching Considerations

Use this blank bookshelf to reflect on books you might like to include in your teaching this month.

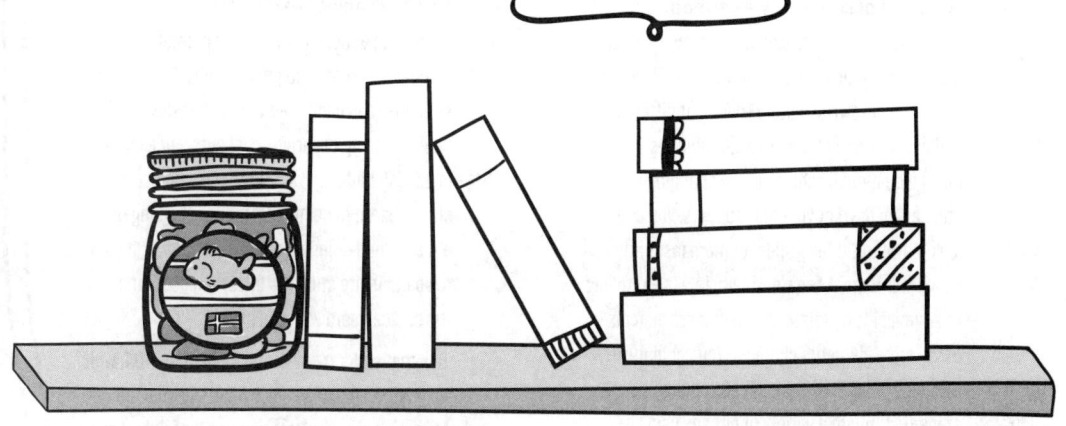

Title	Author and Illustrator	Teaching Considerations

Activities and Instructional Moves

Follow the invitations to help share this month's theme with your classroom. You'll find invitations and instructional guidance for elementary (K–5) and intermediate (6–8) students.

Kindergarten to Fifth Grade

- **Write a choose-your-own-adventure story:** Invite your students to explore their own version of a choose-your-own-adventure story. They may write or rewrite a story trying out different endings and considering new possibilities. You may guide them by charting and changing various story elements. For younger students, you can look to fractured fairy tales for more inspiration as mentor texts. A fractured fairy tale is a retelling of a familiar fairy tale with one or more aspects of the story elements changed. You could make a change in point of view, or you could guide students through a variety of options using a story map. Searching for "fractured fairy tales" online will take you to many helpful resources that will guide you through planning a lesson (readwritethink.org has a particularly helpful classroom resources page). Students have fun creating their own stories by choosing what happens next, which helps them understand how stories are put together.

- **Create a choice board:** Assemble a choice board with a menu of options to promote independent work and provide opportunities for students to expand their thinking or show their understanding of various concepts. For example, in English language arts, students can use a choice board to demonstrate their thinking about a read-aloud or independent book choice. It's up to you to invite students to participate in making the choice board with you or not.

  See the reader menu template in figure 10.1, which will help you build a choice board for yourself or your students. Students can use these choice boards to select their own reading-based activity, which can help them feel empowered in their own exploration of a text. Figure 10.2 shows a sample choice board based on this template.

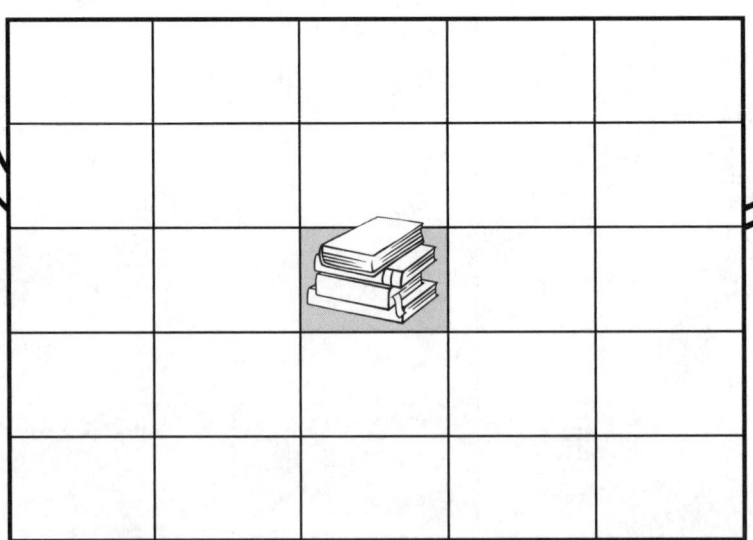

FIGURE 10.1: Reader menu template.

*Visit **go.SolutionTree.com/literacy** for a free reproducible version of this figure.*

Explain how one of the characters reminds you of someone you know.	Compare and contrast yourself to a character in the book by completing a T-chart. Include three similarities and three differences.	Where and when does the story take place? Describe with plenty of detail.	Illustrate one of the characters from your story.
Make a text-to-self, text-to-text, or text-to-world connection to the book.	Discuss one of the problems in the story and tell how you think it will be solved.	What events caused you to feel the following emotions: fear, sadness, joy, anger, and hope? Explain.	Draw a detailed map that shows the setting of the story.
Create a collage for the story. Include pictures and words. On the back, tell why you picked each picture or word.	Find song lyrics that represent a character in your story. Copy the lyrics and tell why you picked them.	Make a character web for one of the main characters in the book. Include seven traits and supporting examples.	Write down three facts and one opinion about the book.

FIGURE 10.2: Sample choice board.

Sixth to Eighth Grade

- **Write a choose-your-own-adventure story:** Have students write a story with at least three different outcomes for characters based on the choices they make. This means students will have to write at least three different endings. With each ending, students must make sure the protagonists learn different lessons and that the reader has the opportunity to make several different choices throughout the story. As a bonus, students might use an online tool (like www.twinery.org) to make their stories even more interactive.

- **Reflect on an important decision:** Have students think about a time when they made an important decision. Ask, "How would your life be different if you had chosen differently?" Then, have students create a short story or comic strip that explores both versions of life based on the outcomes of the decision. What would have happened in the alternate version of their life? Feel free to encourage students to involve magical or otherworldly elements like a mentor, trickster, or fairy godmother that will help them explore the realm of possibilities.

End-of-Month Reflection Questions

1. In what ways have your views on personalized learning, choice activities, and student-centered lessons been strengthened, shifted, or challenged?

   _____
   _____
   _____

2. In what ways do your school's halls and walls celebrate the unlimited talents of your students? What messages do they send?

   _____
   _____
   _____

3. What lessons might you want to share that have taught you to believe in what's possible?

   _____
   _____
   _____

4. What lessons have your young learners taught you that connect passions, practice, and perseverance to what's possible?

   _____
   _____
   _____

5. How do your classrooms and lessons help students view all that is possible? What reinforces those ideas? What might you need to explore further?

   _____
   _____
   _____

JUNE

Play and Rest

Play is often talked about as if it were a relief from serious learning. But for children, play is serious learning.

—Fred Rogers

Research shows that play is the best form of self-care. It can be a vital tool for maintaining mental health and emotional resilience (Edwards, 2023). Together, play and rest are essential components of our well-being and forms of self-care. This reciprocal relationship contributes to a healthier and more fulfilling community of learners. Through play, children learn how to build connections, manage emotions, navigate conflicts, and even self-advocate. Play can also foster a love for learning, creativity, communication, and self-expression; it can also enrich individuals' lives and promote a joyful sense of agency and autonomy. There's something special about those sounds and sights at recess. In addition to the joy of seeing universal signs of smiles and laughter, free play and play-based learning are important ways we learn about the world. Let's make room for play.

Important Dates

- Caribbean American Heritage Month
- Rainbow Book Month
- Audio Book Appreciation Month
- Pride Month
- Immigrant Heritage Month
- National Oceans Month
- Juneteenth (June 19)

Looking Ahead: July

- Disability Pride Month
- National Park and Recreation Month

JUNE

To Do

Notes

Monday	Tuesday	Wednesday
○	○	○
○	○	○
○	○	○
○	○	○
○	○	○

Thursday	Friday	Saturday	Sunday
○	○	○	○
○	○	○	○
○	○	○	○
○	○	○	○
○	○	○	○

Inspiration

In *Purposeful Play: A Teacher's Guide to Igniting Deep and Joyful Learning Across the Day*, educators Kristi Mraz, Alison Porcelli, and Cheryl Tyler (2016) offer significant research to support the power of play, concluding that play is what keeps us thriving as people. We agree with these scholars and believe we all need to make space for work *and* play! So, this month, take the time to do what you love . . . or not do anything at all. Be intentional about the steps you can take to refresh your mind, body, and spirit. Rest. Relax. Feed your spirit. Invite your students to reflect on the many ways we can play and learn together. Look to Mraz and colleagues' (2016) book *Purposeful Play* or consider viewing the TED Talk "Play Is More than Just Fun" by Stuart Brown (2008), founder of the National Institute for Play, to extend the conversation on the power of play.

Illumination

Here, you have a chance to explore play and rest in your own life. Use the invitations below to engage meaningfully with this month's theme and reflect on what it means to you.

1. Think back to a time when you first learned something new. In what ways did play have a role?

    _____
    _____
    _____

2. How does your classroom reflect the many ways we can play and learn together, as a group and as individuals?

    _____
    _____
    _____

3. What activities do you engage in to refresh your mind? Your body? Your Spirit?

    _____
    _____
    _____

4. Who or what helps you prioritize your own self-care?

    _____
    _____
    _____

5. What do you think would benefit your students in prioritizing more play-based activities? What could you do to reduce stress as they explore new learning?

    _____
    _____
    _____

6. Consider opportunities for literacy play. Where do you incorporate play in word study? Mathematics? Science? Health? Social studies? Where might you add more and how?

    _____
    _____
    _____

Investigation

Investigate this month's theme of play and rest with your students by inviting them to complete the following activities. Think and talk about ways you can inspire play and rest with your text choices.

Kindergarten to Fifth Grade

In our research, we learned that the first Saturday of every month has been named National Play Outside Day (www.playoutsideday.org). Think about the possibilities. Encourage your students to make a list of all the ways they might play outside and challenge them to complete that list over the course of this month.

Sixth to Eighth Grade

Have students respond to this prompt and complete the tasks in a journal entry: "When thinking about the ways we rest and play, consider how much time you dedicate to each. Make a clock and separate it into times for rest, learning, work, and play. How many hours do you allocate to each? Do some research into another part of the world or country that interests you. How do people spend their time there or divide the hours in their day? What similarities do you see? What's different?"

Mentor Spotlight: Bettina Love

Bettina Love is a cofounder of the Abolitionist Teaching Network and author of the books *We Want to Do More Than Survive* (2019) and *Punished for Dreaming: How School Reform Harms Black Children and How We Heal* (2023). Love is an "education abolitionist" with the goal of abolishing the harmful status quo within educational institutions and practices. Her work explores the interplay between action and observation. Love is an acute scholar of the power dynamics at play in education that keep young people, particularly young Black students, from being able to experience play and rest at school. She reminds us that learning for all students should be joyful rather than another obstacle they must overcome to survive.

As Love's biography on her personal website states, her practice is rooted in "abolitionist teaching, anti-racism, Hip-Hop education, Black girlhood, queer youth, educational reparations, and the use of art-based education to foster youth civic engagement" (Love, 2023). As you read Love's books and learn from her, consider individuals in your community who might be able to experience a more liberatory and uplifting experience by incorporating the ideals she teaches educators to learn more about and potentially adopt as their own.

Visit Bettina Love's website using the following QR code.

www.bettinalove.com

Week One

To Do

Notes

Monday

Tuesday

Wednesday

In order to move forward to a more equitable world, we must wobble so that we can topple what oppresses and marginalizes us. Without the wobbles, therefore, we can't expect change to happen.

—Antero Garcia and Cindy O'Donnell-Allen

Thursday

Friday

Saturday

Sunday

Week Two

To Do

Notes

Monday

Tuesday

Wednesday

Reading is not just a hobby, it is a lifelong passion that can ignite your imagination and fuel your dreams.

— **LeVar Burton**

Thursday

Friday

Saturday

Sunday

Week Three

To Do

Notes

Monday

Tuesday

Wednesday

> You were not just born to center your entire existence on work and labor. You were born to heal, to grow, to be of service to yourself and community, to practice, to experiment, to create, to have space, to dream, and to connect.
>
> —Tricia Hersey

Thursday

Friday

Saturday

Sunday

Week Four

To Do

Notes

Monday

Tuesday

Wednesday

Rest isn't a reward for work; it's part of the work.

—Leesa Renée Hall

Thursday

Friday

Saturday

Sunday

June Bookshelves

Title	Author and Illustrator	Teaching Considerations
Breathe (2014)	Scott Magoon	This whale's tale serves as a tool to explore many life lessons. With its encouraging reminder to take the time to breathe, love, and be loved, it will be a cherished read-aloud for all.
How to Bird (2023)	Rasha Hamid	This photo essay and procedural text will invite young explorers to learn from the wonderful outdoors. The essay also serves as a great mentor text for informational writing.
Let's Play: Children's Games From Around the World (2023)	Nancy Dickmann, illustrated by Mónica Andino	Share this illustrated informational guide all about play. Your students will learn about an array of games, cultures, and traditions.
Playtime for Restless Rascals (2022)	Nikki Grimes, illustrated by Elizabeth Zunon	This book celebrates family and playtime. Share this book to spark conversations about what play means to your students.
Today (2024)	Gabi Snyder, illustrated by Stephanie Graegin	With backmatter for mindfulness exercises, your students will reflect on the everyday moments and matters that make up their days.
The Very Inappropriate Word (2013)	Jim Tobin, illustrated by Dave Coverly	This read-aloud book can provide the perfect opportunity to reflect on the importance of being mindful about the words we use. It is also a great way to expand students' vocabulary and knowledge about words.
We All Play (2021)	Julie Flett	With a glossary of Cree words, this picture book looks at the connections between humans, animals, nature, and play. It also provides an opportunity to explore movement in actions and words.

248

Title	Author and Illustrator	Teaching Considerations
Merci Suárez Changes Gears (2020)	Meg Medina	Merci Suárez has a lot of new experiences entering middle school. She also has a lot of hobbies she loves. Use this novel to teach about holding on to the people and things we love when everything we think we know about the world around us changes.
Robot Dreams (2016)	Sara Varon	This wordless graphic novel about a dog and a robot is a poignant story about the nature of friendship. Use it to teach about self-discovery through rest and play with companions we choose and adventures that choose us.
The Season of Styx Malone (2019)	Kekla Magoon	Caleb and his younger brother Bobby Gene befriend a new kid in town with an adventurous game to play and some intriguing secrets to unveil. Use this text to teach about lessons that can be learned outside the school year and in the most surprising relationships.
The Strange Case of Origami Yoda (2015)	Tom Angleberger	A sixth grader makes a small origami puppet that he suspects might be anthropomorphic. The book makes connections between play, art, and navigating middle school, and readers might decide to try learning origami (the book contains instructions).
We Still Belong (2024)	Christine Day	Wesley Wilder is a gamer and member of the Upper Skagit tribe. She wants to ask her crush to the school dance, but things don't go exactly as planned. Teach about gaming as a form of connection across lived experiences and cultures with this coming-of-age tale.

June Bookshelves

Title	Author and Illustrator	Teaching Considerations

Use this blank bookshelf to reflect on books you might like to include in your teaching this month.

Title	Author and Illustrator	Teaching Considerations

Activities and Instructional Moves

Follow the invitations to help share this month's theme with your classroom. You'll find invitations and instructional guidance for elementary (K-5) and intermediate (6-8) students.

Kindergarten to Fifth Grade

- **Enact vocabulary time:** Make time for students to explore vocabulary by experimenting and playing with words. Inspire word play and visual art by inviting students to create drawings or sentences that use context clues to better illustrate meaning.
- **Create illustrated words:** You may also suggest that your students provide a visual display of words and their meanings using word art sites like Canva, Word Art, Word Cloud, WordItOut, and Word Swag, just to name a few. Jim Tobin's (2013) *The Very Inappropriate Word*, one of the book selections on this month's Bookshelves pages (pages 248-249) includes some sample ideas for this activity. See figure 11.1 for an example.

FIGURE 11.1: Illustrated words.

- **Use poetry for craft:** Invite your students to choose a piece of poetry. They may select a favorite poem or one of their own pieces to rewrite, changing words or fonts, or reorganizing the poem's white space to experiment further for more literacy play.

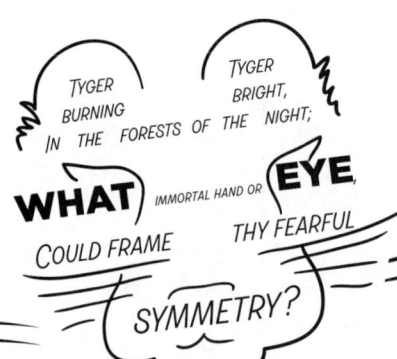

Sixth to Eighth Grade

- **Dedicated rest and relaxation time:** Create a rest and relaxation activity for those in your class or learning community. These could be coloring pages, sticker by number, needlepoint, doing puzzles, or anything else you can think of that encourages relaxation. After a week of engaging in the activity every day for at least twenty minutes, have students journal about how the experience has changed their days. As a bonus, make a gallery for your school displaying the projects everyone created.

- **Create your own board game:** Have students create a board game in groups of no more than four. Then, host a day where everyone plays the games that others in the class created. The games should have rules, they may have game pieces, and there should be clear ways to determine a winner or winners. Students might consider using a game that already exists (like Monopoly) and just changing the setting or pieces. Remind students about card games or games that involve no pieces at all (like Twister). Ask students to document the process so they can share what they learned. And have fun!

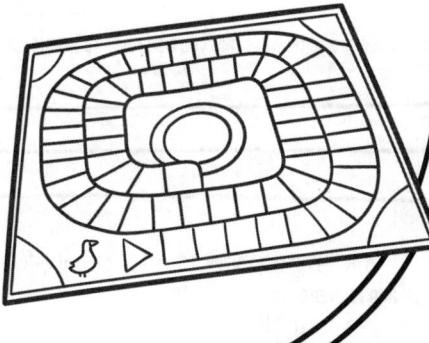

End-of-Month Reflection Questions

1. What does playful learning mean to you?

   _____
   _____
   _____

2. What does playful learning look like? Feel like?

   _____
   _____
   _____

3. How does your environment promote playful learning?

   _____
   _____
   _____

4. What are some ways that you find rest? Your students?

   _____
   _____
   _____

5. How does your reflection on play and rest feel different now? In what ways does it aid in your own self-care and rejuvenation?

   _____
   _____
   _____

JULY

Imagination

Writing and reading are not all that distant for a writer. Both exercises require being alert and ready for unaccountable beauty, for the intricateness or simple elegance of the writer's imagination, for the world that imagination evokes.

—Toni Morrison

How lucky are educators to have a cyclical year of instruction? Educators approach each school year with a fresh start and end-of-year routines allow for reflection on what a gift it is to have an imagination. As readers, we can use our imagination to experience new things, new people, and new places, both real and fictional. As writers, we can share our own stories and create our own endings. Interpretation would not exist without imagination. Through literacy, we can expand our imagination and dream bigger and better. These patterns of learning and reflection are essential for growth. So, whether you are ready to embark on your newest year of teaching or wrapping up the current one and thinking about what was, we encourage you to embrace the optimism that comes with this journey of learning as lifework. Imagine the possibilities when we make the most of every moment.

Important Dates

- Disability Pride Month
- National Park and Recreation Month
- National Ice Cream Month
- Read an Almanac Month
- National Graphic Novels Month
- Independence Day (July 4)
- National Parents' Day (fourth Sunday of July)
- International Day of Friendship (July 30)
- Paperback Book Day (July 30)

Looking Ahead: August

- Back to School Month
- International Peace Month
- National Inventors Month

JULY

To Do

Notes

Monday	Tuesday	Wednesday
○	○	○
○	○	○
○	○	○
○	○	○
○	○	○

Thursday	Friday	Saturday	Sunday
○	○	○	○
○	○	○	○
○	○	○	○
○	○	○	○
○	○	○	○

Inspiration

When we imagine, we believe that something is possible. Imagination leads to creation, and it also demonstrates our ability to strengthen our knowledge and experiences. When we read, we use our imagination to make inferences, expand our perspectives, and gain new insights. In addition to enhancing imagination, reading can encourage creativity, deepen understanding, and lead to new discoveries. Reading is essential to connect imagination, play, and learning. It's central to what we know and how we shape our experiences, real or imagined. As you think about this school year and all those moments that shaped your community of learners, may you continue on your journey of reflective practice, purposeful planning, centering students, literacy celebrations, and book joy. And as you continue to grow in your own cycle of self-discovery, keep imagining, keep exploring, and celebrate what you have created in this year of planning with us.

Illumination

Here, you have a chance to explore imagination in your own life. Use the invitations below to engage meaningfully with this month's theme and reflect on what it means to you.

1. What helps you to strengthen your imagination?

2. How might you incorporate more opportunities for imaginative role play, fictional writing, or storytelling? Where and when might you add that?

3. In what ways does your imagination deepen your connection to texts? To others?

4. Who are some people from your community who you believe will not be forgotten?

5. How might your ability to imagine others' experiences (actual or hypothetical) increase your understanding?

6. Which do you think matters more, imagination or knowledge? Why? How do you see their connections?

Investigation

Investigate this month's theme of imagination with your students by inviting them to complete the following activities. Think and talk about ways you can inspire imagination with your text choices.

Kindergarten to Fifth Grade

We can extend our ideas when we engage our imaginations. Invite your students to complete the following two sentences or expand on its ideas: "Imagine if . . ." or "If I were a _____." For younger students, brainstorm a list of possibilities to guide them ("if I were a dog," "if I were a tree," or our personal favorite, "if I were a book"). Ask older students to incorporate similes or metaphors as they build on this imaginative scene in play, art, or using their words.

Sixth to Eighth Grade

Imagination is an important part of creating the world we want to live in. Some of the most celebrated works of literature take place in fictional worlds and comment on the real world. Have students investigate some of the most famous science fiction and fantasy authors. Then, ask students the following questions.

- What do these authors have in common?
- How are they different?
- What are some of the recurring themes and archetypes in their works?

Mentor Spotlight: Kwame Alexander

Kwame Alexander is an educator, poet, award-winning author of over forty books for young people (and those who serve them), and executive producer, showrunner, and writer of Emmy Award-winning Disney+ series *The Crossover* (2023).

Alexander's books *The Undefeated* (2019), *The Door of No Return* (2022), *An American Story* (2023), and *Black Star* (2024) reimagine the past for readers and, along the way, restore dignity and humanity to African Americans by telling the full story of how Africans were brought to the Americas and what happened to them after they arrived. Alexander weaves the past and present together with lyric poetry and with emotionally resonant artwork, reimagining what Americans have been told about the past to move us toward a better, more inclusive future.

Alexander regularly shares his passion for literacy, books, and writing at events around the world. In Ghana, he is well known for opening the Barbara E. Alexander Memorial Library and Health Clinic.

Visit Kwame Alexander's website using the following QR code.

www.kwamealexander.com

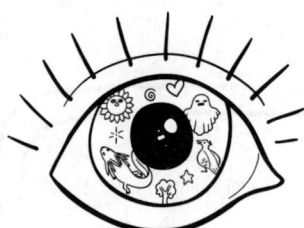

Week One

To Do

Notes

Monday

Tuesday

Wednesday

We read books to find out who we are. What other people, real or imaginary, do and think and feel. . . is an essential guide to our understanding of what we ourselves are and may become.

—Ursula K. Le Guin

Thursday

Friday

Saturday

Sunday

Week Two

To Do

Notes

Monday

Tuesday

Wednesday

> The monks teach that we mere mortals cannot question fate. But I say that we control destiny by our every action. Our power lies in the choices we make.
>
> —Ellen Oh

Thursday

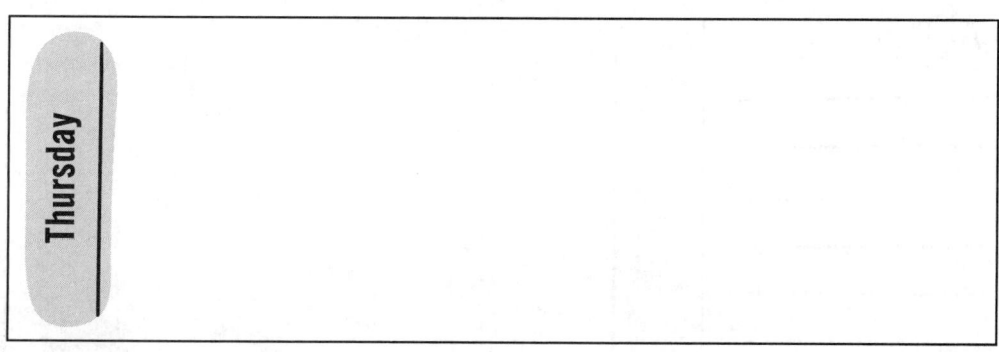

Friday

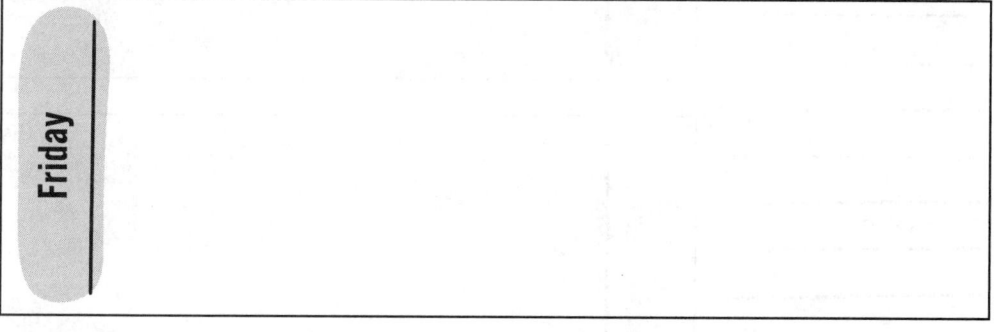

Saturday

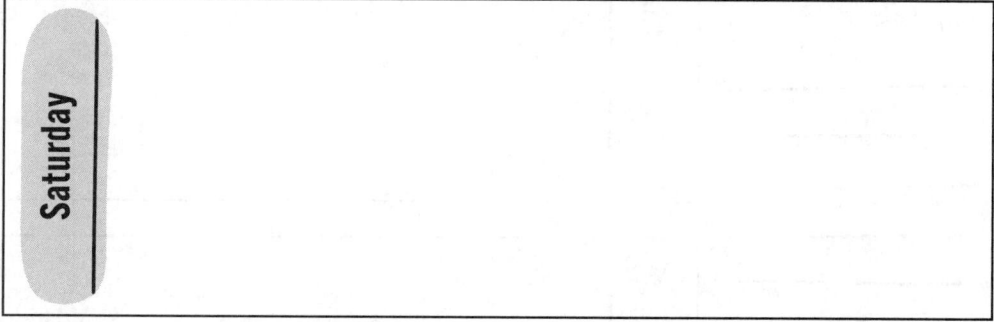

Sunday

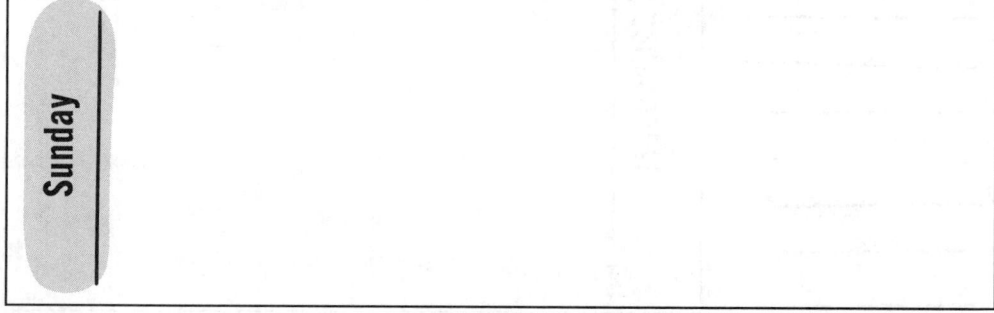

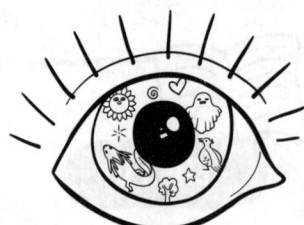

Week Three

To Do

Notes

Monday

Tuesday

Wednesday

Magic is an expression of the unlimited capacity of mystery and wonder in the world.

—**Melissa de la Cruz**

Thursday

Friday

Saturday

Sunday

Week Four

To Do

Notes

Monday

Tuesday

Wednesday

It's the spider's web, an old African symbol for creativity and wisdom. It shows how tangled and complicated life can be. But with a little imaginative thinking, we can solve most of our problems and those of others.

—Kwame Mbalia

Thursday

Friday

Saturday

Sunday

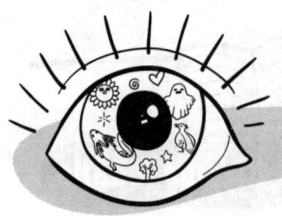

July Bookshelves

Title	Author and Illustrator	Teaching Considerations
Every Day's a Holiday: Winnie's Birthday Countdown (2023)	Stef Wade, illustrated by Husna Aghniya	Read aloud to explore a variety of traditions, honor an array of holidays, and imagine what would happen if we made the most of everyday celebrations.
I Wonder (2019)	Kari Anne Holt, illustrated by Kenard Pak	Share this text to invite questions, spark investigations, and connect wonder and imagination.
Partly Cloudy (2024)	Deborah Freedman	This hybrid text provides opportunities to explore varying perspectives and interpretations. It also teaches about clouds and the water cycle.
When You Take a Step (2022)	Bethanie Deeney Murguia	Read this text to invite conversations about being open minded, taking risks, and knowing that new steps lead to new discoveries.
Why Not? A Story About Discovering Our Bright Possibilities (2024)	Kobi Yamada, illustrated by Gabriella Barouch	This is another inspirational text by Yamada that explores complex questions and will again leave readers inspired to imagine what's possible and in their reach.

Title	Author and Illustrator	Teaching Considerations
The Door of No Return (2022)	Kwame Alexander	In this novel in verse about a young boy living in precolonial West Africa, readers will find the humanity in those who have historically been dehumanized and reimagine what they think they know about Black history before enslavement.
A Snake Falls to Earth (2024)	Darcie Little Badger	Use this dual-narrative tale to teach about spirituality, the world beyond the natural world, and themes of climate change, identity, and family.
Tristan Strong Punches a Hole in the Sky (2020)	Kwame Mbalia	Use this beautifully crafted tale to teach about world-building and using the imagination to transform the world we live in—especially if dealing with more difficult emotions like survivor's guilt or grief and loss.
Where the Mountain Meets the Moon (2019)	Grace Lin	Teach about a hero's quest and the role of traditional folklore in inspiring modern audiences to tap into their inner superpowers.
A Wish in the Dark (2021)	Christina Soontornvat	In this middle-grade novel about morality and oppression, a dash of magic adds intrigue and adventure to teach lessons about social justice and personal power.

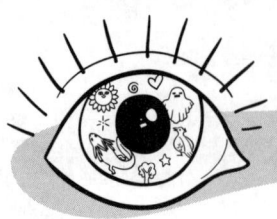

July Bookshelves

Title	Author and Illustrator	Teaching Considerations

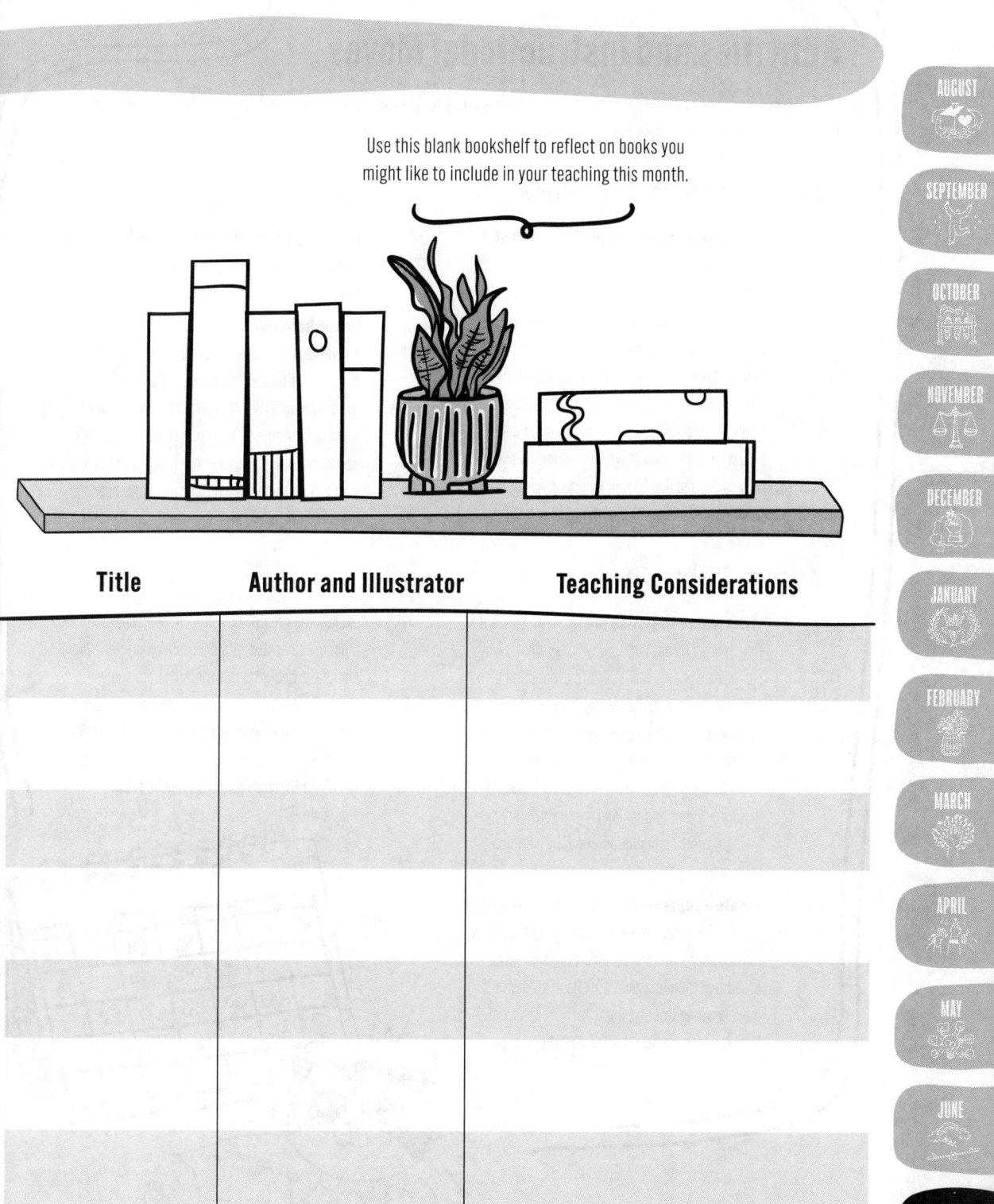

Use this blank bookshelf to reflect on books you might like to include in your teaching this month.

Title	Author and Illustrator	Teaching Considerations

Activities and Instructional Moves

Follow the invitations to help share this month's theme with your classroom. You'll find invitations and instructional guidance for elementary (K-5) and intermediate (6-8) students.

Kindergarten to Fifth Grade

- **Create your own calendar:** Think about all the ways we can kick off the new year with a celebratory lens. Imagine we could create our own calendar of holidays for our unique community of learners. Inspired by Stef Wade's (2023) *Every Day's a Holiday* and in honor of the fact that there is something to celebrate every day, invite students to discuss, draw, or write about a new holiday that they would wish to celebrate. Make a class list and add to your calendar. As you prepare to get to know the students in this new class, suggest they include their birthdays, family traditions, and cultural celebrations in the list to ensure that all are celebrated.

- **Be the book!** Ask your students to think about a favorite text or select a read-aloud from our suggested titles on this month's Bookshelves pages (pages 270-271). Invite students to work alone or in groups to choose a character, favorite scene, or setting and then use imaginative role play, acting their chosen topic as in charades, for others to guess the book mystery.

Sixth to Eighth Grade

- **Write a fact-to-fiction piece:** Writing science fiction and fantasy isn't always easy. That's why sometimes people take real-life events and give them a small twist, like adding fantasy characters or changing a setting to a place that would seem impossible to visit. Have students try their hand at world-building by taking an ordinary place or historical event and making it extraordinary by changing setting or characters or by adding a little magic.

- **Create a superhero trailer:** Part of the reason people like superheroes so much is because they remind us that humans are only limited by the breadth of their imaginations. Have students make a trailer by stitching together clips from their favorite movies or animated shows that explain the greatness of the chosen superhero. As a bonus, have students choose a character from one of the books on this month's Bookshelves pages (pages 270-271) and make a short video explaining why the character they chose qualifies as a hero. They may refer to Joseph Campbell's (1949/2008) classic hero's cycle or create their own.

End-of-Month Reflection Questions

1. Reflect on the accomplishments and the challenges you and your students faced throughout the year. What went well?

   _____
   _____
   _____

2. Also reflecting on the past year, what could have been improved? What do you hope to do again and how might you adjust to improve even further?

   _____
   _____
   _____

3. How have you grown personally and professionally this school year?

   _____
   _____
   _____

4. Identify the most important goals you have for the new school year. What are you most excited about and why?

   _____
   _____
   _____

5. Consider sharing your goals with a colleague. Who will you support? Who will you turn to for support?

   _____
   _____
   _____

6. What do you imagine will help you create the best year yet?

   _____
   _____
   _____

FAREWELL

As you wrap up your final season with this guide, we hope it will inspire you to move forward with a refreshed view of literacy and your role as a literacy educator. The works we have included represent more than one season of learning and discovery. They represent many years of reading, writing, and learning alongside young people that have inspired us with their perseverance and curiosity. Love of literature doesn't come easily to everyone. But, for those of us who have always loved reading and writing, we know how fulfilling it can be to find yourself in the pages of a new and undiscovered title. It is important to remember that inside every young person is a reader, and that reading lives transform throughout the seasons of a person's life, and that is OK. Encourage the young people in your community to build reading lives and identities rooted in their interests and life experiences, not necessarily those of the established status quo or society that surrounds them. Remind them that any season is a good time to fall in love with a good book and rediscover yourself along the way.

Jo Ellen   *Julia E. Torres*

REFERENCES AND RESOURCES

Adichie, C. N. (2009, July). *The danger of a single story* [Video]. TED Conferences. Accessed at https://www.ted.com/talks/chimamanda_ngozi_adichie_the_danger_of_a_single_story on February 11, 2025.

Affirmation. (n.d.). In *Oxford English dictionary*. Accessed at https://www.oed.com/search/dictionary/?scope=Entries&q=affirmation on February 11, 2025.

Akiwenzie-Damm, K., Assu, S., Mitchell, B., Qitsualik-Tinsley, R., Qitsualik-Tinsley, S., Robertson, D. A., et al. (2019). *This place: 150 years retold*. Winnipeg, MB, Canada: HighWater Press.

Alexander, K. (2019). *The undefeated*. New York: Versify.

Alexander, K. (2021). *Out of wonder*. Somerville, MA: Candlewick Press.

Alexander, K. (2022). *The door of no return*. New York: Little, Brown.

Alexander, K. (2023). *An American story*. New York, NY: Little, Brown.

Alexander, K. (2024). *Black star*. New York: Little, Brown.

Alexander, K., Carter, M., Henderson, J. James, L., Johnson, A., Johnson, D., et al. (Executive Producers). (2023). *The crossover* [TV series]. Magicworthy; Big Sea Entertainment; SpringHill Entertainment; State St. Pictures; 20th Television; Disney Branded Television.

Ali, A. E. (2020). *Our favorite day of the year*. New York: Salaam Reads.

Allyn, P., & Morrell, E. (2023, March 13). Telling our own tales. *Language Magazine*. Accessed at www.languagemagazine.com/2023/03/13/telling-our-own-tales on September 6, 2024.

American Legal Association. (n.d.). *Diversity heritage months.* ALA Gateway. Accessed at https://ala-gateway.org/Diversity_Heritage_Months on January 14, 2025.

American Library Association. (2007). *Library celebration days.* Accessed at https://www.ala.org/conferencesevents/celebrationdays on January 14, 2025.

American Library Association (2023). *TeenTober.* Accessed at https://www.ala.org/aasl/advocacy/promo/TeenTober on January 14, 2025.

Amnesty International. (2015). *Dreams of freedom in words and pictures.* London: Frances Lincoln Children's Books.

Angleberger, T. (2015). *The strange case of origami Yoda.* New York: Abrams.

Archer, M. (2021). *Wonder walkers.* New York: Nancy Paulsen Books.

Atwell, N. (2002). *Lessons that change writers.* Portsmouth, NH: Heinemann.

Baptiste, T. (2015). *The jumbies.* Chapel Hill, NC: Algonquin Young Readers.

Barbosa, B. (2020). *I am! Affirmations for resilience.* New York: Penguin.

Barnes, D. (2020). *I am every good thing.* New York: Nancy Paulsen Books.

Bayron, K. (2023). *The vanquishers.* New York: Bloomsbury.

Bender, M. (2021). *The end is just the beginning.* New York: Random House.

Bildner, P. (2021). *High five for Glenn Burke.* New York: Square Fish.

Birdsong, B. (2019). *I will be fierce.* New York: Roaring Brook Press.

Bourne, S., & Levy, D. A. (2022). *Allies: Real talk about showing up, screwing up, and trying again.* New York: DK Children.

Bowles, D. (2021). *They call me Güero: A border kid's poems.* New York: Kokila.

Brady, A. (2021, April 2). *The history (and present) of banning books in America.* Literary Hub. Accessed at https://lithub.com/the-history-and-present-of-banning-books-in-america on February 11, 2025.

Brosgol, V. (2021). *Memory jars.* New York: Roaring Brook Press.

Brown, S. (2008). *Play is more than just fun* [Video]. TED Conferences. Accessed at https://www.ted.com/talks/stuart_brown_play_is_more_than_just_fun?subtitle=en on February 12, 2025.

Browne, M. L. (2016). *Black girl magic.* New York: Roaring Brook Press.

Bruchac, J. (2022). *Rez dogs.* New York: Dial Books.

Byers, G. (2018). *I am enough.* New York: Balzer and Bray.

Callender, K. (2022). *King and the dragonflies.* New York: Scholastic.

Campbell, J. (2008). *The hero with a thousand faces* (3rd ed.). Novato, CA: New World Library. (Original work published 1949)

Cervantes, A. (2020). *Lety out loud.* New York: Scholastic.

Chavez, F. R. (2021). *The antiracist writing workshop: How to decolonize the creative classroom.* Chicago: Haymarket Books.

Chmakova, S. (2017). *Brave.* New York: Yen Press.

Christensen, L. (2017). *Reading, writing, and rising up: Teaching about social justice and the power of the written word* (2nd ed.). Milwaukee, WI: Rethinking Schools Ltd.

Christmas, J. (2022). *Swim team.* New York: HarperAlley.

Cisneros, E. (2023). *Falling short.* New York: HarperCollins.

Colagiovanni, M. (2024). *The reflection in me.* New York: Scholastic.

Craft, A. (2021). *Treaty words: For as long as the rivers flow.* Toronto, Ontario, Canada: Annick Press.

Dalton, A. (2022). *Show the world!* New York: Penguin.

Davies, N. (2020). *Every child a song: A celebration of children's rights.* New York: Hachette.

Day, C. (2024). *We still belong.* New York: Heartdrum.

Dembicki, M. (Ed.). (2021). *Trickster: Native American tales—A graphic collection* (10th anniversary ed.). Chicago: Chicago Review Press.

Dewey, J. (1997). *Experience and education.* New York: Free Press.

Dickmann, N. (2023). *Let's play: Children's games from around the world.* London: Words and Pictures.

DiTerlizzi, A. (2020). *The magical yet.* New York: Little, Brown.

DiTerlizzi, A. (2024). *The curious why.* New York: Little, Brown.

Douglass, F. (2016). *Narrative of the life of Frederick Douglass, an American slave.* Minneapolis: Anboco. (Original work published 1845)

Dubosh, E., Poulakis, M., & Abdelghani, N. (2015). Islamophobia and law enforcement in a post 9/11 world. *Islamophobia Studies Journal, 3*(1), 138–157. https://doi.org/10.13169/islastudj.3.1.0138

The Editors of Encyclopaedia Britannica (1998, July 20). *Cycle.* Encyclopedia Britannica. Accessed at https://www.britannica.com/art/cycle-literature on May 2, 2025.

Edwards, A. (n.d.). *What is One Little Word®?* Accessed at https://aliedwards.com/one-little-word-2024 on February 10, 2025.

Edwards, D. (2023). *Play—The best form of self-care*. BHMA. Accessed at https://bhma.org/play-the-best-form-of-self-care/#:~:text=The%20research%20is%20clear%2C%20play,with%20improved%20ways%20of%20coping on January 14th, 2025.

Elhillo, S. (2022). *Home is not a country*. New York: Make Me a World.

Emmons, R. A. (2019). Joy: An introduction to this special issue. *The Journal of Positive Psychology, 15*(1), 1–4. https://doi.org/10.1080/17439760.2019.1685580

Fisher, L. (2023). *Friends beyond measure*. New York: HarperCollins.

Flett, J. (2021). *We all play*. Vancouver, British Columbia, Canada: Greystone.

Fox, M. (2017). *Wilfrid Gordon McDonald Partridge* (40th anniversary ed.). New York: Scholastic. (Original work published 1984)

Freedman, D. (2024). *Partly cloudy*. New York: Penguin.

Garcia, A. (n.d.). *At the heart of what I do—as a researcher, writer, teacher, and dreamer—is a relentless pursuit of freedom and justice*. Accessed at https://anterogarcia.com/ on February 11, 2025.

Garcia, A. & O'Donnell-Allen, C. (2015). *Pose wobble flow: A culturally proactive approach to literacy instruction*. New York: Teachers College Press.

Giles, L. (2020). *The last mirror on the left*. New York: Versify.

González, X. (2023). *Remembering*. New York: Simon & Schuster.

Gorman, A. (2021). *Change sings: A children's anthem*. New York: Penguin.

Gorman, A. (2023). *Something, someday*. New York: Penguin.

Gray, G. R., Jr. (2023). *I'm from*. Toronto, ON, Canada: Tundra Books.

Grimes, N. (2022). *Playtime for restless rascals*. Naperville, IL: Sourcebooks.

Guerrero, D., & Moroz, E. (2019). *My family divided: One girl's journey of home, loss, and hope*. New York: Square Fish.

Gutman Library. (2024). *Book banning in the United States and beyond*. Harvard Graduate School of Education. Accessed at https://guides.library.harvard.edu/c.php?g=1269000&p=9306840 on February 6, 2025.

Hamid, R. (2023). *How to bird*. Minneapolis: Free Spirit Publishing.

Hammond, Z. (2014). *Culturally responsive teaching and the brain: Promoting authentic engagement and rigor among culturally and linguistically diverse students*. Thousand Oaks, CA: Corwin.

Handy, B. (2023). *What if one day . . .* New York: Enchanted Lion Books.

Harjo, J. (1996). *The woman who fell from the sky: Poems* (Revised ed.). New York: Norton.

Harste, J. C. (2021). *Researching literate lives: The selected work of Jerome C. Harste*. New York: Routledge.

Hermanns, K. (2017, February 14). *"Justice is what love looks like in public"* [Blog post]. Accessed at https://pridefoundation.org/2017/02/justice-is-what-love-looks-like-in-public on September 9, 2024.

Hernandez, C. (2020). *Sal and Gabi break the universe*. New York: Disney Hyperion.

Hindley, A. F. (2019). *A is for all the things you are: A joyful ABC book*. Washington, DC: Smithsonian Books.

Hiranandani, V. (2019). *The night diary*. New York: Kokila.

Holt, K. A. (2019). *I wonder*. New York: Random House Children's Books.

Hopson, N. R. (2023). *Eagle drums*. New York: Roaring Brook Press.

Hunt, L. M., & Carpenter, N. (2025). *Wish in a tree*. Nancy Paulsen Books.

Iyer, D. (2017). *Social change ecosystem map*. Building Movement Project. Accessed at buildingmovement.org/our-work/movement-building/social-change-ecosystem-map on November 13th, 2024.

James, L. (2020). *I promise*. New York: HarperCollins.

Johnson, V. (2018). *The Parker inheritance*. New York: Scholastic.

Johnston, P. H. (2012). *Opening minds: Using language to change lives*. Portland, ME: Stenhouse.

Johnston, P. H. (2024). *Choice words: How our language affects children's learning* (2nd ed.). New York: Routledge.

Kahn, H. (2017). *Amina's voice*. New York: Simon & Schuster.

Kapp, D. (2022). *Girls who green the world: Thirty-four rebel women out to save our planet*. New York: Delacorte.

Kelly, E. E. (2020). *Lalani of the distant sea*. New York: Greenwillow Books.

Kelly, E. E. (2024). *The first state of being*. New York: Greenwillow Books.

Keselman, A. (2003). Supporting inquiry learning by promoting normative understanding of multivariate causality. *Journal of Research in Science Teaching, 40*(9), 898–921. https://DOI:10.1002/tea.10115

Khorram, A. (2019). *Darius the great is not okay*. New York: Penguin.

Kim, J. (2020). *Stand up, Yumi Chung*. New York: Kokila.

Kleon, A. (2012). *Steal like an artist: 10 things nobody told you about being creative*. New York: Workman.

LaRocca, R. (2021). *Red, white, and whole.* New York: Quill Tree Books.

Latham, I., & Waters, C. (2020). *Dictionary for a better world: Poems, quotes, and anecdotes from A to Z.* Minneapolis: Carolrhoda Books.

Lavelle, K. (2023). *Butt or face?* Naperville, IL: Sourcebooks.

Lê, M. (2018). *Drawn together.* New York: Little, Brown.

Lê, M. (2020). *Green Lantern: Legacy.* Burbank, CA: DC Comics.

Lê, M. (2023). *Enlighten me.* New York: Little, Brown.

León, A (2020). *Freedom, we sing.* London: Flying Eye Books.

Lin, G. (2019). *Where the mountain meets the moon.* New York: Little, Brown.

Little Badger, D. (2024). *A snake falls to earth.* Hoboken, NJ: Levine Querido.

Love, B. L. (2019). *We want to do more than survive: Abolitionist teaching and the pursuit of educational freedom.* Boston: Beacon Press.

Love, B. L. (2023). *Punished for dreaming: How school reform harms Black children and how we heal.* New York: St. Martin's Press.

MacArthur Foundation. (2020). *Jacqueline Woodson.* Accessed at https://www.macfound.org/fellows/class-of-2020/jacqueline-woodson on February 5, 2025.

Magoon, K. (2019). *The season of Styx Malone.* New York: Yearling.

Magoon, S. (2014). *Breathe.* New York: Simon & Schuster.

Maldonado, T. (2021). *What lane?* New York: Nancy Paulsen Books.

Marks, J. (2021). *From the desk of Zoe Washington.* New York: Katherine Tegen Books.

Marter, J. (2023, July 13). *Discovering your glimmers: Finding moments of joy.* Choosing Therapy. Accessed at https://www.choosingtherapy.com/glimmers/ on January 13th, 2025.

Maynor, M. (2021). *A house for every bird.* New York: Knopf.

Mbalia, K. (2020). *Tristan Strong punches a hole in the sky.* New York: Disney Hyperion.

McLernon, L. M. (2024, May 22). 5 questions with author Joanna Ho. *Mpls.St.Paul Magazine.* Accessed at https://mspmag.com/arts-and-culture/5-questions-with-author-joanna-ho/ on February 10, 2025.

Medina, J. (2022). *I am! A book of reminders.* New York: Versify.

Medina, M. (2020). *Merci Suárez changes gears.* Somerville, MA: Candlewick Press.

Miller, C. (2018, September 6). *Reimagining the canon to study youth culture.* NCTE. Accessed at https://ncte.org/blog/2018/06/reimagining-the-canon-to-study-youth-culture/ on January 21, 2025.

Miller, D. (2009). *The book whisperer: Awakening the inner reader in every child.* San Francisco: Jossey-Bass.

Mitchell, M. (2021). *My very favorite book in the whole wide world.* New York: Scholastic.

Moniuszko, S. M. (2022, March 29). "Glimmers" are the opposite of triggers. Here's how to embrace them. *USA Today.* Accessed at https://www.usatoday.com/story/life/health-wellness/2022/03/23/glimmers-opposite-triggers-mental-health-benefits/7121353001/ on January 21, 2025.

Mora, O. (2018). *Thank you, Omu!* New York: Little, Brown.

Mora, O. (2019). *Saturday.* New York: Little, Brown.

Moraga, C., & Anzaldúa, G. (2015). *This bridge called my back: Writings by radical women of color* (4th ed.). Albany, NY: State University of New York Press.

Morera, J., & Encarnación, V. (2025). *Together we remember.* New York: Make Me A World.

Morrison, T., & Morrison, S. (2014). *Please, Louise.* New York: Simon & Schuster.

Mraz, K., Porcelli, A., & Tyler, C. (2016). *Purposeful play: A teacher's guide to igniting deep and joyful learning across the day.* Portsmouth, NH: Heinemann.

Muhammad, G. (2021). *Cultivating genius: An equity framework for culturally and historically responsive literacy.* New York: Scholastic.

Muhammad, G. (2023). *Unearthing joy: A guide to culturally and historically responsive teaching and learning.* New York: Scholastic.

Muhtaris, K., Ziemke, K., & Harvey, S. (2015). *Amplify: Digital teaching and learning in the K–6 classroom.* Portsmouth, NH: Heinemann.

Murguia, B. D. (2022). *When you take a step.* New York: Beach Lane Books.

Myers, M. (2021). *Not little.* New York: Holiday House.

National Council of Teachers of English. (2025, January 7). *Intellectual Freedom Center.* Accessed at https://ncte.org/resources/ncte-intellectual-freedom-center/ on January 21, 2025.

National Day Calendar. (2025). *National day calendar—fun, unusual and forgotten designations on our calendar.* Accessed at https://nationaldaycalendar.com on May 2, 2025.

Nichols, D. (2021). *Art of protest: Creating, discovering, and activating art for your revolution.* New York: Big Picture Press.

Noë, S. A. (2024, January 17). *2023 literary and book-themed holidays for your calendar.* Accessed at https://onthecobblestoneroad.com/book-themed-holidays-2023 on February 11, 2025.

Nuño, F. (2017). *The map of good memories.* Madrid, Spain: Cuento de Luz.

Oshiro, M. (2022). *You only live once, David Bravo.* New York: HarperCollins.

Otheguy, E. (2020, September 14). Children's books and contradictions. *The Horn Book.* Accessed at https://www.hbook.com/story/childrens-books-and-contradictions on September 6, 2024.

Otoshi, K., & Baumgarten, B. (2015). *Beautiful hands.* New York: Gosling Books.

Paquette, A.-J., & Thompson, L. A. (2017). *Two truths and a lie: It's alive!* New York: HarperCollins.

Parker, T. (1853). *Ten sermons of religion.* Boston: Crosby, Nichols, and Company.

Paul, M. (Ed.). (2019). *Thanku: Poems of gratitude.* Minneapolis: Millbrook Press.

Pedaste, M., Mäeots, M., Leijen, Ä., & Sarapuu, S. (2012). Improving students' inquiry skills through reflection and self-regulation scaffolds. *Technology, Instruction, Cognition and Learning, 9,* 81–95.

Pedaste, M., Mäeots, M., Siiman, L. A., de Jong, T., van Riesen, S. A. N., Kamp, E. T., et al. (2015). Phases of inquiry-based learning: Definitions and the inquiry cycle. *Educational Research Review, 14,* 47–61. https://doi.org/10.1016/j.edurev.2015.02.003

Pember, M. (2019, December 19). *"Decolonise and re-indigenise": The Ojibwe language warrior.* Aljazeera. Accessed at www.aljazeera.com/features/2019/12/19/decolonise-and-re-indigenise-the-ojibwe-language-warrior on June 14, 2024.

PEN America. (2025). *PEN America index of school book bans—2023–2024.* Accessed at https://pen.org/book-bans/pen-america-index-of-school-book-bans-2023-2024 on February 10, 2025.

Pérez, C. C. (2018). *The first rule of punk.* New York: Puffin Books.

Peters, M. A. (2014). Socrates and Confucius: The cultural foundations and ethics of learning. *Educational Philosophy and Theory, 47*(5), 423–427. https://doi.org/10.1080/00131857.2014.930232

Pippins, A. (2024). *The spark in you.* New York: Random House.

Prasadam-Halls, S. (2020). *Rain before rainbows.* Somerville, MA: Candlewick Press.

Reynolds, J. (2017). *Ghost.* New York: Atheneum Books.

Rhuday-Perkovich, O. (2022). *Operation sisterhood.* New York: Crown.

Richardson, M. S. (2024). *Five words that are mine.* Naperville, IL: Sourcebooks.

Robinson, R. (2023). *This book is my best friend.* New York: Simon & Schuster Books for Young Readers.

Robles, L. (n.d.). *Blackout poetry* [Lesson plan]. Accessed at https://www.lerobles.com/uploads/4/7/8/5/4785749/blackout_poetry_lesson_plan_1.pdf on February 11, 2025.

Rosenthal, A. K. (2007). *The OK book.* New York: HarperCollins.

Sainte-Marie, B. (2022). *Still this love goes on.* Vancouver, British Columbia, Canada: Greystone.

Salazar, A. (2022). *A seed in the sun.* New York: Dial Books.

Sang, M. M. (2021). *Mindset changes everything* [Video]. Ted Conferences. Accessed at https://www.ted.com/talks/may_may_sang_mindset_changes_everything_jan_2021?subtitle=en on September 9, 2024.

Sass, A. J. (2021). *Ana on the edge.* New York: Little, Brown.

Shraya, V. (2016). *The boy & the bindi.* Vancouver, British Columbia, Canada: Arsenal Pulp Press.

Siddiqui, M. (2022). *Barakah beats.* New York: Scholastic.

Singer, M. (2018). *Every month is a new year: Celebrations around the world.* New York: Lee & Low Books.

Smith, C. R., Jr. (2013). *I am a poet* [Video]. YouTube. Accessed at https://www.youtube.com/watch?v=MU1lK0H9JtE on February 11, 2025.

Smith, N. (2023). *The artivist.* New York: Kokila.

Smith, N. (2024). *The artivist by Nikkolas Smith—Promo* [Video]. YouTube. Accessed at https://youtu.be/L0k0xlY044Q on February 6, 2025.

Smith, T., & Barnes, D. (2022). *Victory. Stand! Raising my fist for justice.* New York: Norton.

Snyder, G. (2024). *Today.* New York: Simon & Schuster.

Soontornvat, C. (2021). *A wish in the dark.* Somerville, MA: Candlewick Press.

Sorell, T. (2021). *We are still here! Native American truths everyone should know.* Watertown, MA: Charlesbridge.

Souto-Manning, M., & Martell, J. (2016). *Reading, writing, and talk: Inclusive teaching strategies for diverse learners, K–2.* New York: Teachers College Press.

Stead, T. (2014). Nurturing the inquiring mind through the nonfiction read-aloud. *The Reading Teacher, 67*(7), 488-495.

Stevenson, B. (2019). *Just mercy: A true story of the fight for justice (adapted for young adults).* New York: Ember.

Stewart, M. (2020a). *Nonfiction writers dig deep: 50 award-winning children's book authors share the secret of engaging writing.* Champaign, IL: NCTE.

Stewart, M. (2020b). *Pipsqueaks, slowpokes, and stinkers: Celebrating animal underdogs.* Atlanta, GA: Peachtree.

Stewart, M., & Chesley, N. (2014). *Perfect pairs: Using fiction & nonfiction picture books to teach life science, K–2.* New York: Routledge.

Stewart, M., & Chesley, N. (2016). *Perfect pairs: Using fiction & nonfiction picture books to teach life science, 3–5.* New York: Routledge.

Stewart, M., & Correia, M. P. (2023). *5 kinds of nonfiction: Enriching reading and writing instruction with children's books.* New York: Routledge.

Takei, G., Eisinger, J., & Scott, S. (2019). *They called us enemy.* San Diego, CA: Top Shelf Productions.

Talbott, H. (2021). *A walk in the words.* New York: Nancy Paulsen Books.

Tallie, M. E. (2019). *Layla's happiness.* New York: Enchanted Lion Books.

Tatum, A. W. (2009). *Reading for their life: (Re)building the textual lineages of African American adolescent males.* Portsmouth, NH: Heinemann.

Tobin, J. (2013). *The very inappropriate word.* New York: Henry Holt.

Treuer, A. (2021). *Everything you wanted to know about Indians but were afraid to ask: Young readers edition.* Hoboken, NJ: Levine Querido.

Tyson, N. D. (2016). *StarTalk: Everything you ever need to know about space travel, sci-fi, the human race, the universe, and beyond.* Washington, DC: National Geographic.

VanDerwater, A. L. (2017). *Read! Read! Read!* Honesdale, PA: Wordsong.

VanDerwater, A. L. (2020). *Write! Write! Write!* Honesdale, PA: Wordsong.

Varon, S. (2016). *Robot dreams.* New York: Square Fish.

Venkatraman, P. (2023). *Born behind bars.* New York: Nancy Paulsen Books.

Verde, S. (2023). *Who I am: Words I tell myself.* New York: Abrams.

Vourvoulias, S. (2020). *Nuestra América: 30 inspiring Latinas/Latinos who have shaped the United States.* New York: Running Press.

Wade, C. (2021). *What the road said.* New York: Feiwel and Friends.

Wade, S. (2023). *Every day's a holiday: Winnie's birthday countdown.* New York: Hachette.

Watson, R. (2021). *Ways to make sunshine.* London: Bloomsbury.

Watson, R. (2022). *Where you from?* [Video]. YouTube. Accessed at https://www.youtube.com/watch?v=av_7CA9PmsU on February 11, 2025.

Wilkins, E. J. (2023). *Zora the story keeper*. New York: Penguin.

Witek, J. (2016). *All my treasures: A book of joy*. New York: Abrams.

Woodson, J. (2016). *Brown girl dreaming*. New York: Puffin Books.

Woodson, J. (2022). *Before the ever after*. New York: Nancy Paulsen Books.

Yamada, K. (2021). *Maybe: A story about the endless potential in all of us*. Seattle: Compendium.

Yamada, K. (2024). *Why not? A story about discovering our bright possibilities*. Seattle: Compendium.

Yamasaki, K. (2021a). *Katie Yamasaki*. Accessed at https://www.katieyamasaki.com/theartist on January 21, 2025.

Yamasaki, K. (2021b). *Dad bakes*. New York: Norton.

Yang, G. L. (2013). *Boxers*. New York: First Second.

Yang, K. (2019). *Front desk*. New York: Scholastic.

Yoo, P. (2024). *Rising from the ashes: Los Angeles, 1992. Edward Jae Song Lee, Latasha Harlins, Rodney King, and a city on fire*. New York: Norton.

Yousafzai, M. (2017). *Malala's magic pencil*. New York: Little, Brown.

Zoboi, I. (2022). *Star child: A biographical constellation of Octavia Estelle Butler*. New York: Dutton.

INDEX

A

A Is for All the Things You Are (Hindley), 48
acceptance, 16
Acevedo, E., 23
activist identity, 98
activities and instructional moves, 7
    on affirmation, 208–209
    on belonging, 30–31
    on calling, 142
    on imagination, 274
    on joy, 52, 74–75
    on justice, 98
    on liberation, 164
    on play and rest, 252–253
    on possibility, 230–231
    on remembrance, 120
    on renewal, 186–187
Adichie, C. N., 194
affirmation, 189–210
    activities and instructional moves for, 208–209
    bookshelves on, 204–207
    definition of, 190
    to do pages for, 192–193
    illumination on, 194
    important dates and, 191
    inspiration for, 194
    investigation on, 195
    mentor spotlight for, 195
    reflection questions on, 210
    weekly spreads for, 196–203
affirmation stations, 208
affirmation walls, 209
agency, 212, 216, 234
Akiwenzie-Damm, K., 205
Alexander, K., 70, 94, 261, 271
Ali, A. E., 26
Ali, M., 111
All My Treasures (Witek), 48
Allende, I., 181
Allies (Bourne & Levy), 27
Allyn, P., 41
American Library Association, 82
An American Story (Alexander), 94, 261
Amina's Voice (Kahn), 27
Amnesty International, 160, 164
Ana on the Edge (Sass), 205
Angelou, M., 45, 225
Angleberger, T., 249
The Antiracist Writing Workshop (Chavez), 151
Anzaldúa, G., 7
April, 189–210
    activities and instructional moves for, 208–209
    bookshelves for, 204–207
    to do pages for, 192–193
    illumination for, 194
    important dates in, 191

inspiration for, 194
investigation for, 195
mentor spotlight for, 195
reflection questions for, 210
weekly spreads for, 196–203
Archer, M., 70
Art of Protest (Nichols), 161
The Artivist (Smith), 98
Assu, S., 205
attitude, 168
August
    bookshelves, 26–29
    to do pages, 14–15
    illumination in, 16
    important dates in, 13
    inspiration in, 16
    investigation in, 17
    mentor spotlight for, 17
    reflection questions on, 32
    weekly spreads, 18–25
autonomy, 234

B

Badger, D. L., 271
Baldwin, J., 145
Baptiste, T., 71
Barakah Beats (Siddiqui), 49
Barbosa, B., 204
Barnes, D., 26, 117
Baumgarten, B., 94
Bayron, K., 71
Beautiful Hands (Otoshi), 94
Before the Ever After (Woodson), 183
belonging, 11–32
    bookshelves for, 26–29
    definition of, 12
    to do pages on, 14–15
    illumination and, 16
    important dates, 13
    inspiration and, 16
    investigation on, 17
    mentor spotlight for, 17
    reflection questions on, 32
    weekly spreads for, 18–25
Bender, M., 226
Bhutto, B., 78
Bildner, P., 49
Birdsong, B., 26

Black Girl Magic (Browne), 209
Black Star (Alexander), 261
blackout poems, 209
board games, creating, 253
book bannings, 82
The Book Whisperer (Miller), 142
bookshelves, 7
    on affirmation, 204–207
    on belonging, 26–29
    on calling, 138–141
    on imagination, 270–273
    on joy, 48–51
    on justice, 94–97
    on liberation, 160–163
    on play and rest, 248–251
    on possibility, 226–229
    on remembrance, 116–119
    on renewal, 182–185
Born Behind Bars (Venkatraman), 95
Bourne, S., 27
Bowles, D., 161
Boxers (Yang), 161
The Boy & the Bindi (Shraya), 204
Brave (Chmakova), 27
Breathe (Magoon), 248
Brosgol, V., 117
Brown, A. M., 167
Brown, B., 201
Brown, S., 238
Browne, M. L., 209
Bruchac, J., 49
Buck, P. S., 219
Burke, T., 197
Burton, L., 243
Butler, O. E., 221
Butt or Face? (Lavelle), 70
Byers, G., 26

C

calendars, creating your own, 274
Callender, K., 205
calling, 123–143
    activities and instructional moves on, 142
    bookshelves on, 138–141
    to do pages on, 126–127
    illumination on, 128
    important dates and, 125

inspiration on, 128
reflection questions on, 143
weekly spreads on, 130–137
career choices. *See* calling
celebration, 5–6
of joy, 52
Cervantes, A., 139
change. *See* renewal
Chavez, F. R., 151
Chesley, N., 61
Chmakova, S., 27
choice boards, 230–231
Choice Words (Johnston), 186
choose-your-own adventure stories, 230, 231
Chopra, D., 131
Christensen, L., 31
Christmas, J., 205
Cisneros, E., 183
Clarke, A. C., 211
Colagiovanni, M., 138
collaboration, 7–8
community spaces, 31
confidence, belonging and, 12
Correia, M., 61
Corrin, A., 160
Craft, A., 183
The Crossover, 261
Cruz, M. de la, 267
Cultivating Genius (Muhammad), 39
The Curious Why (DiTerlizzi), 226

D

Dad Bakes (Yamasaki), 204
Dalton, A., 138
The Danger of a Single Story (Adichie), 194
Darius the Great Is Not Okay (Khorram), 183
Davies, N., 160
Day, C., 249
December, 101–121
activities and instructional moves for, 120
bookshelves for, 116–119
to do pages for, 104–105
illumination for, 106
important dates in, 103
inspiration for, 106
investigation in, 107
mentor spotlight in, 107

reflection questions for, 121
weekly spreads for, 108–115
decisions, reflecting on, 231
deGrasse Tyson, N., 71
Dembicki, M., 227
Dewey, J., 109
DiCamillo, K., 43
Dickmann, N., 248
Dictionary for a Better World (Latham & Waters), 26
DiTerlizzi, A., 226
The Door of No Return (Alexander), 261, 271
Douglass, F., 146
Drawn Together (Lê), 107
Dreams of Freedom in Words and Pictures (Amnesty International), 160, 164

E

Eagle Drums (Hopson), 117
Edelman, M. W., 137
Edwards, A., 142
Eisinger, J., 95
Elhillo, S., 161
Emmons, R. A., 34
Encyclopedia Britannica, 187
The End Is Just the Beginning (Bender), 226
end-of-month reflections, 7
on affirmation, 210
on belonging, 32
on imagination, 275
on inquiry, 76
on joy, 53
on justice, 99
on liberation, 165
on play and rest, 254
on possibility, 232
on remembrance, 121
on renewal, 188
Enlighten Me (Lê), 107
environments
of belonging, 12
joyful, 34, 38
Every Child a Song (Davies), 160
Every Day's a Holiday (Wade), 270, 274
Every Month is a New Year (Singer), 138
Everything You Wanted to Know About Indians but Were Afraid to Ask (Treuer), 71

F

fact-to-fiction writing, 274
Falling Short (Cisneros), 183
February, 145–165
    activities and instructional moves for, 164
    bookshelves for, 160–163
    to do pages for, 148–149
    illumination in, 150
    important dates in, 147
    inspiration in, 150
    investigation in, 151
    mentor spotlight in, 151
    reflection questions for, 165
    weekly spreads for, 152–159
The First Rule of Punk (Pérez), 161
The First State of Being (Kelly), 227
Fisher, L., 70
Five Words That Are Mine (Richardson), 204
5 Kinds of Nonfiction (Stewart & Correia), 61
Flett, J., 248
found poems, 52
Fox, M., 116
Freedman, D., 270
freedom. *See* liberation
Freedom, We Sing (León), 160
Freire, P., 60
Friends Beyond Measure (Fisher), 70
From the Desk of Zoe Washington (Marks), 95
Front Desk (Yang), 139

G

gallery walks, 52
Garcia, A., 217, 241
Ghandi, M., 78
Ghost (Reynolds), 49
Giles, L., 227
Girls Who Green the World (Kapp), 183
glitter boards, 31
González, X., 116
Gorman, A., 94, 138
Gray, G. R., Jr., 204, 208
Green Lantern: Legacy (Lê), 107
Grimes, N., 248
Guerrero, D., 95

H

Haaland, D., 78
Hall, L. R., 247
Hamid, R., 248
Hammond, Z. L., 65
Handy, B., 160
Harjo, J., 93, 175
Harste, J. C., 69
Hernandez, C., 139
Hersey, T., 245
A High Five for Glenn Burke (Bildner), 49
Hindley, A. F., 48
Hiranandani, V., 117
history. *See* remembrance
Ho, J., 129, 133
holidays, 6
Holmes, E., 70
Holt, K. A., 270
Home Is Not a Country (Elhillo), 161
hooks, b., 87
Hopson, N. R., 117
A House for Every Bird (Maynor), 48
How to Bird (Hamid), 248
Huerta, D., 179
Hunt, L. M., 70
Hurston, Z. N., 67

I

I Am! Affirmations for Resilience (Barbosa), 204
I Am Enough (Byers), 26
I Am Every Good Thing (Barnes), 26
I Promise (James), 26
I Will Be Fierce (Birdsong), 26
I Wonder (Holt), 270
illumination, 6
    on affirmation, 194
    belonging and, 16
    on calling, 128
    on imagination, 260
    on inquiry, 60
    joy and, 38
    on justice, 83
    on liberation, 150
    on play and rest, 238
    on possibility, 216

on remembrance, 106
on renewal, 172
illustrated words, 252
I'm From (Gray), 204, 208
imagination, 255–275
    activities and instructional moves on, 274
    bookshelves on, 270–273
    to do pages on, 258–259
    illumination on, 260
    important dates and, 257
    inspiration on, 260
    mentor spotlight on, 261
    reflection questions on, 275
    weekly spreads for, 262–269
important dates, 6
    April, 191
    August, 13
    December, 103
    February, 147
    January, 125
    July, 257
    June, 235
    March, 169
    May, 213
    November, 79
    October, 57
    September, 35
inclusion, 5, 12
inquiry, 55–76
    activities and instructional moves on, 74–75
    bookshelves on, 70–73
    definition of, 55
    to do pages for, 58–59
    illumination for, 60
    important dates and, 57
    inspiration for, 60
    investigation of, 61
    mentor spotlight on, 61
    reflection questions on, 76
    weekly spreads for, 62–69
insights. *See* illumination
inspiration, 5–6
    on affirmation, 194
    on belonging, 16
    on calling, 128
    on imagination, 260
    on inquiry, 60
    on joy, 38
    on liberation, 150
    on play and rest, 238
    on possibility, 216
    on remembrance, 106
    on renewal, 172
Intellectual Freedom Center, 82
investigation, 6–7
    on affirmation, 195
    of belonging, 17
    on calling, 129
    on imagination, 261
    on inquiry, 61
    on joy, 39
    of justice, 84
    on play and rest, 239
    on possibility, 217
    of remembrance, 107
    on remembrance, 107
    on renewal, 173
Iyer, D., 124

J

James, L., 26
January, 123–143
    activities and instructional moves, 142
    bookshelves for, 138–141
    to do pages for, 126–127
    illumination in, 128
    important dates in, 125
    inspiration in, 128
    investigation in, 129
    mentor spotlight in, 129
    reflection questions for, 143
    weekly spreads for, 130–137
Jemison, M., 55
Johnson, V., 71
Johnston, P., 186
joy, 33–53
    activities and instructional moves for, 52
    bookshelves on, 48–51
    definition of, 34
    to do pages for, 36–37
    illumination on, 38
    important dates and, 35

inspiration on, 38
investigating, 39
mentor spotlight on, 39
reflection questions on, 53
July, 255–275
    activities and instructional moves for, 274
    bookshelves for, 270–273
    to do pages for, 258–259
    illumination for, 260
    important dates in, 257
    inspiration for, 260
    investigation for, 261
    mentor spotlight for, 261
    reflection questions for, 275
    weekly spreads for, 262–269
The Jumbies (Baptiste), 71
June, 233–254
    activities and instructional moves for, 252–253
    bookshelves for, 248–251
    to do pages for, 236–237
    illumination for, 238
    important dates in, 235
    inspiration for, 238
    investigation for, 239
    mentor spotlight for, 239
    reflection questions for, 254
    weekly spreads for, 240–247
Just Mercy (Stevenson), 95
justice, 77–99
    activities and instructional moves for, 98
    bookshelves on, 94–97
    definition of, 78
    to do pages for, 80–81
    illumination on, 83
    important dates and, 79
    inspiration on, 82
    investigation of, 84
    mentor spotlight on, 85
    reflection on, 99
    weekly spreads for, 86–93

K

Kaba, M., 203
Kahn, H., 27
Kapp, D., 183
Kelly, E. E., 139, 227
Khorram, A., 183
Kim, J., 49
King, M. L., Jr., 78, 91
King and the Dragonflies (Callender), 205
Kleon, A., 123

L

Lalani of the Distant Sea (Kelly), 139
language, thinking about, 186
LaRocca, R., 27
The Last Mirror on the Left (Giles), 227
Latham, I., 26
Lavelle, K., 70
Layla's Happiness (Tallie), 48
Lê, M., 107, 139
Le Guin, U. K., 263
León, A., 160
Let's Play (Dickmann), 248
letters to your future self, 120
Lety Out Loud (Cervantes), 139
Levy, D. A., 27
liberation, 145–165
    activities and instructional moves on, 164
    bookshelves on, 160–163
    to do pages on, 148–149
    illumination on, 150
    important dates and, 147
    inspiration on, 150
    investigation on, 151
    mentor spotlight on, 151
    reflection questions on, 165
    weekly spreads for, 152–159
Library Bill of Rights, 82
Lin, G., 271
literacy, 277
    building lifelong relationships with, 5–9, 212
    liberation through, 146
    remembering what drew you to, 124
    shared understanding through, 102, 106
    well-being and, 190
Lorde, A., 177
Love, B., 239

M

Magoon, K., 249
Magoon, S., 248
Malala's Magic Pencil (Yousafzai), 160
Maldonado, T., 27
Mandela, N., 78
The Map of Good Memories (Nuño), 116
maps of myself, 120
March, 167–188
    activities and instructional moves for, 186–187
    bookshelves for, 182–185
    to do pages for, 170–171
    illumination for, 172
    important dates in, 169
    inspiration for, 172
    investigation for, 173
    mentor spotlight for, 173
    reflection questions for, 188
    weekly spreads for, 174–181
marginalization, 12
Marks, J., 95
Marley, B., 78
Martell, J., 21
May, 211–232
    activities and instructional moves for, 230–231
    bookshelves for, 226–229
    to do pages for, 214–215
    illumination for, 216
    important dates in, 213
    inspiration for, 216
    investigation in, 217
    mentor spotlight for, 217
    reflection questions for, 232
    weekly spreads for, 218–225
Maybe (Yamada), 226
Maynor, M., 48
Mbalia, K., 269, 271
Medina, J., 204
Medina, M., 249
memory. *See* remembrance
memory jars, 120
Memory Jars (Brosgol), 117
mental health, 234
mentor spotlights, 7
    on affirmation, 195
    on belonging, 17
    on calling, 129
    on imagination, 261
    on inquiry, 61
    on joy, 39
    on justice, 85
    on play and rest, 239
    on possibility, 217
    on remembrance, 107
    on renewal, 173
mentoring, 78
Merci Suárez Changes Gears (Medina), 249
Middle Ground Book Fest, 52
Miller, D., 142
Mitchell, B., 205
Mitchell, M., 48
monthly overviews, 6
Mora, O., 94, 182
Morera, J., 116
Moroz, E., 95
Morrell, E., 41
Morrison, S., 182
Morrison, T., 157, 182, 255
Morton, T., 82
Mount Vernon, 75
Mraz, K., 238
Muhammad, G., 39, 47
multivoice poems, 31
Murguia, B. D., 270
Museum of the Future, 75
My Family Divided (Guerrero & Moroz), 95
My Very Favorite Book in the Whole Wide World (Mitchell), 48
Myers, M., 138
mysteries, investigating, 75

N

National Council of Teachers of English, 82
National Institute for Play, 238
neighborhood polls, 164
nervous system, 38
New English Canaan (Morton), 82
Nichols, D., 161
The Night Diary (Hiranandani), 117
Nonfiction Writers Dig Deep (Stewart), 61
Not Little (Myers), 138
November, 77–99
    activities and instructional moves for,

98
    bookshelves for, 94–97
    to do pages for, 80–81
    illumination in, 83
    important dates in, 79
    inspiration on, 82
    investigation in, 84
    mentor spotlight in, 85
    reflection questions for, 99
    weekly spreads for, 86–93
Nuestra América (Vourvoulias), 205
Nuño, F., 116

O

October, 55–76
    activities and instructional moves, 74–75
    bookshelves for, 70–73
    to do pages for, 58–59
    illumination for, 60
    important dates in, 57
    inspiration for, 60
    investigation in, 61
    mentor spotlight for, 61
    reflection questions, 76
    weekly spreads for, 62–69
O'Donnell-Allen, C., 241
Office for Intellectual Freedom, 82
Oh, E., 265
The OK Book (Rosenthal), 182
Opening Minds (Johnston), 186
Operation Sisterhood (Rhuday-Perkovich), 49
Oshiro, M., 227
Otheguy, E., 25
Otoshi, K., 94
Our Favorite Day of the Year (Ali), 26
Out of Wonder (Alexander & Holmes), 70
Oxford English Dictionary, 190

P

Paquette, A.-J., 226
Parker, T., 83
The Parker Inheritance (Johnson), 71
Parks, R., 101
Partly Cloudy (Freedman), 270
passion, exploring your, 142
Paul, M., 85, 94
Pérez, C. C., 161

Perfect Pairs (Chesley & Stewart), 61
personal growth, reflecting on, 120
Pippins, A., 138
Pipsqueaks, Slowpokes, and Stinkers (Stewart), 26
play and rest, 233–254
    activities and instructional moves on, 252–253
    bookshelves on, 248–251
    to do pages on, 236–237
    illumination on, 238
    important dates and, 235
    inspiration on, 238
    investigation on, 239
    mentor spotlight on, 239
    reflection questions on, 254
    weekly spreads on, 240–247
"Play Is More than Just Fun" (Brown), 238
Playtime for Restless Rascals (Grimes), 248
Please, Louise (Morrison & Morrison), 182
poems
    blackout, 209
    found, 52
    multivoice, 31
    shape, 52
poetry crafts, 252
poetry cycles, 187
polling the neighborhood, 164
polyvagal theory, 38
Porcelli, A., 238
positive thinking, 186
possibility, 211–232
    activities and instructional moves for, 230–231
    bookshelves for, 226–229
    to do pages for, 214–215
    illumination for, 216
    important dates and, 213
    inspiration for, 216
    investigation on, 217
    mentor spotlight on, 217
    reflection questions on, 232
    weekly spreads for, 218–225
practices and pedagogies. *See* investigation
Prasadam-Halls, S., 182
Punished for Dreaming (Love), 239
purpose. *See* calling
purpose, finding your, 142
Purposeful Play (Mraz, Porcelli, & Tyler), 238

Q

Qitsualik-Tinsley, R., 205
Qitsualik-Tinsley, S., 205
quote boxes and quote collages, 30

R

Rain Before Rainbows (Prasadam-Halls), 182
Read! Read! Read! (VanDerwater), 48
Reading, Writing, and Rising Up (Christensen), 31
recommendations. *See* bookshelves
Red, White, and Whole (LaRocca), 27
reflection. *See also* end-of-month reflections
    on art, 98
    on calling, 143
    on important decisions, 231
The Reflection in Me (Colagiovanni), 138
Remembering (González), 116
remembrance, 101–121
    activities and instructional moves on, 120
    bookshelves for, 116–119
    to do pages for, 104–105
    illumination on, 106
    important dates and, 103
    inspiration on, 106
    investigation on, 107
    mentor spotlight on, 107
    reflection questions on, 121
    weekly spreads for, 108–115
renewal, 167–188
    activities and instructional moves on, 186–187
    bookshelves on, 182–185
    to do pages for, 170–171
    illumination on, 172
    important dates and, 169
    inspiration on, 172
    investigation on, 173
    mentor spotlight for, 173
    reflection questions on, 188
    weekly spreads for, 174–181
resilience, 234
resolutions, 142
resources. *See* bookshelves
rest. *See* play and rest
Reynolds, J., 49, 199
Rez Dogs (Bruchac), 49
Rhuday-Perkovich, O., 49
Richardson, M. S., 204
Riley, C. A., 159
Rising from the Ashes (Yoo), 117
Robinson, R., 182
Robot Dreams (Varon), 249
Rogers, F., 233
Roosevelt, E., 113
Rosenthal, A. K., 182

S

Sal and Gabi Break the Universe (Hernandez), 139
Salazar, A., 117
Sang, M. M., 186
Sass, A. J., 205
Saturday (Mora), 182
scaffolding, 9
school, studying your, 187
Scott, S., 95
The Season of Styx Malone (Magoon), 249
A Seed in the Sun (Salazar), 117
self-care. *See* play and rest
September, 33–53
    activities and instructional moves, 52
    bookshelves for, 48–51
    to do pages for, 36–37
    illumination in, 38
    important dates in, 35
    inspiration in, 38
    investigation in, 39
    reflection questions, 53
    reflection questions for, 53
    weekly spreads for, 40–47
service opportunities, 98
Shakur, A., 153
shape poems, 52
Show the World! (Dalton), 138
Shraya, V., 204
Siddiqui, M., 49
Simmons, D., 189
Singer, M., 138
Smith, N., 98
Smith, T., 117
A Snake Falls to Earth (Badger), 271
Snyder, G., 248
Social Change Ecosystem Map, 124
social media campaigns, 98, 164
Something, Someday (Gorman), 138

Soontornvat, C., 271
Sorell, T., 94
Souto-Manning, M., 21
The Spark in You (Pippins), 138
Stand Up, Yumi Chung! (Kim), 49
Star Child (Zoboi), 227
StarTalk (deGrasse Tyson), 71
Stead, T., 75
Stevenson, B., 95
Stewart, M., 26, 61
The Strange Case of Origami Yoda (Angleberger), 249
superhero trailers, 274
Suzuki, S., 223
Swim Team (Christmas), 205

T

Takei, G., 95
Talbott, H., 70
Tallie, M. E., 48
Tatum, A., 19
TED Talks, 186, 194, 238
Texas FReadom Fighters, 82
Thank You, Omu! (Mora), 94
Thanku (Paul), 94
themes, 9
    affirmation, 189–210
    belonging, 11–32
    calling, 123–143
    imagination, 255–275
    inquiry, 55–76
    joy, 33–53
    justice, 77–99
    liberation, 145–165
    play and rest, 233–254
    possibility, 211–232
    remembrance, 101–121
    renewal, 167–188
They Call Me Güero (Bowles), 161
They Called Us Enemy (Takei, Eisinger, & Scott), 95
This Book Is My Best Friend (Robinson), 182
This Place (Akiwenzie-Damm, Assu, Mitchell, Qitsualik-Tinsley, & Qitsualik-Tinsley), 205
Thompson, L. A., 226
Thurman, E., 135
Tobin, J., 248, 252
Today (Snyder), 248
Together We Remember (Morera), 116
Treaty Words (Craft), 183
Treuer, A., 71, 173
Trickster (Dembicki), 227
Tristan Strong Punches a Hole in the Sky (Mbalia), 271
Tum, R. M., 155
Two Truths and a Lie (Paquette & Thompson), 226
Tyler, C., 238

U

The Undefeated (Alexander), 261
Unearthing Joy (Muhammad), 39

V

VanDerwater, A. L., 48
The Vanquishers (Bayron), 71
Varon, S., 249
Venkatraman, P., 95
Verde, S., 204
The Very Inappropriate Word (Tobin), 248, 252
Victory, Stand! (Smith & Barnes), 117
vocabulary time, 252
Vourvoulias, S., 205

W

Wade, C., 226
Wade, S., 270, 274
A Walk in the Words (Talbott), 70
Washington, G., 75
Waters, C., 26
Watson, R., 49
Ways to Make Sunshine (Watson), 49
We All Play (Flett), 248
We Are Still Here! (Sorell), 94
We Need Diverse Books, 85
We Still Belong (Day), 249
We Want to Do More Than Survive (Love), 239
weekly spreads, 7
    April, 196–203
    August, 18–25
    December, 108–115
    February, 152–159
    January, 130–137

July, 262–269
June, 240–247
March, 174–181
May, 218–225
November, 86–93
October, 62–69
September, 40–47
West, C., 89
What If One Day... (Handy & Corrin), 160
What Lane? (Maldonado), 27
What the Road Said (Wade), 226
When You Take a Step (Murguia), 270
Where the Mountain Meets the Moon (Lin), 271
Who I Am (Verde), 204
Why Not? (Yamada), 270
Wilde, O., 115
Wilfrid Gordon McDonald Partridge (Fox), 116
Wilkins, E. J., 116
Williams, P., 33
Wish in a Tree (Hunt), 70
A Wish in the Dark (Soontornvat), 271

Witek, J., 48
Wonder Walkers (Archer), 70
wonder walls, 74
wonder-full investigation, 74
Woodson, J., 11, 17, 183

Y

Yamada, K., 226, 270
Yamasaki, K., 195, 204
Yang, G. L., 161
Yang, K., 139
year at a glance, 6, 9
Yoo, P., 117
You Only Live Once, David Bravo (Oshiro), 227
Yousafzai, M., 77, 160

Z

Ziemke, K., 63
Zoboi, I., 227
Zora, the Story Keeper (Wilkins), 116

Educator Wellness
Timothy D. Kanold and Tina H. Boogren
How do we bring our best selves to our students and colleagues each day? Designed as a reflective journal and guidebook, *Educator Wellness* will take you on a deep exploration where you will uncover profound answers that ring true for you.
BKG053

Leading a Culture of Reading
Lorraine M. Radice
Engaged students achieve better reading success. Grounded in current research, this book provides practical resources and strategies, including the use of technology and social media, that will help educators improve literacy culture in their schools.
BKG124

There's More to the Story
Gwendolyn Cartledge, Amanda L. Yurick, and Alana Oif Telesman
In this valuable resource, the authors share recommendations for diverse and culturally relevant, quality children's literature that explores important aspects of social-emotional learning. In each chapter, book suggestions are paired with activities that promote positive self-reflection and compassionate action toward others.
BKG029

Inspiring Lifelong Readers
Jennifer McCarty Plucker
Grounded in practices that promote adolescent literacy, inquiry, motivation, inspiration, and engagement, Inspiring Lifelong Readers provides secondary teachers with tried-and-true, evidence-based strategies. Discover how you can advance literacy learning so your students become competent, confident, and engaged readers.
BKF947

Solution Tree | Press

Visit SolutionTree.com or call 800.733.6786 to order.

We don't just help schools make a change, we help them *be* the change

REAL IMPACT. RELEVANT SOLUTIONS. RESULTS-DRIVEN APPROACH.

From funding to faculty retention, the evolving demands schools face can be overwhelming. That's where we come in. With professional development rooted in decades of research and delivered by many of the educators who literally wrote the book on it, we empower schools to achieve meaningful change with real, sustainable results.

The change starts here. We can make it happen together.

See how we can get real results for your school or district.

Scan the code or visit:

SolutionTree.com/Results-Driven

 Solution Tree

LET'S SEE WHAT **WE CAN** DO TOGETHER